TEACHER'S GUIDE

My Jewish Year

Celebrating Our Holidays

JESSICA B. WEBER

BEHRMAN HOUSE, INC.
SPRINGFIELD, NEW JERSEY

DEDICATION

FOR DOUG WEBER:
Husband, father, rabbi, and ski aficionado par excellence.

Copyright © 1993 Behrman House, Inc.

Springfield, New Jersey 07081

www.behrmanhouse.com

ISBN 0-87441-541-1

Manufactured in the United States of America

FOREWORD

The Jewish holidays are our vehicles for celebration. We come together on a regular schedule: We prepare for the holiday, we pray, eat, mourn, celebrate—whatever the occasion calls for. At those special times when we are together, we purposefully create "Jewish time." To live a Jewish life in a non-Jewish land we should become comfortable marking off "Jewish time" on the secular calendar, and we must begin doing this from the time we are small.

Adam Fisher's *My Jewish Year* presents the information, the background, and the stories for each of our holidays. But we, the teachers, must provide more. We have to make each of these days real for our students. While we can't teach a person to celebrate, we can assist each family with its celebration by offering information and opportunities to share the holidays together. Our goal is to create memories for the child: memories of meals in the sukkah, the sound of the shofar on Rosh Hashanah, the happy songs sung on Passover. Although it is no easy task, the creation of happy childhood memories is the basic goal of this program.

I hope you enjoy using this Guide. Feel free to use it selectively. Each chapter is full of information as well as ideas for discussion, activities, and projects. Some are simple, others more time consuming. Choose those items with which you feel most comfortable. Keep in mind your own personal teaching style, the nature of your group, and the resources available to you.

Except for longer projects, try to present ideas and information in ten-minute blocks. Vary the lesson by moving from reading, to discussion, to music, to art or drama. To keep the children actively engaged, have many things for them to do.

Younger children like the predictability of a routine. Try to create some format that you follow each week, although within that context you can vary the activities as much as you like. It is nice to open with a blessing, then perhaps give tzedakah, and then move on to introduce the lesson. Using a basic framework, be creative, be full of surprises, and most important, have fun!

CONTENTS

INTRODUCTION
How To Use This Guide

The Structure of the Textbook

The textbook *My Jewish Year* is divided into twelve chapters, one for each of the Jewish holidays. Each chapter includes background information, stories, exercises, and instruction on holiday observance. You can spend several hours of class time on each chapter, depending on the number of activities you choose and the depth of your discussions.

Important Concepts

In each chapter of this Guide, the section entitled "Important Concepts" serves as an outline or overview of the chapter. Concentrate on one or two main ideas at a time in order to plan an effective lesson.

Vocabulary

This section lists the words you may want to introduce to your students before reading the text.

Background Information

This section is intended to add depth to the teacher's understanding of the subject matter. It contains some information for your own edification and some material you may want to share directly with your students.

Introducing the Lesson

This section provides suggestions for introducing the holiday to your students. It sets the stage for the topic and gets students thinking about the issues ahead.

Teaching the Story

Some of the chapters contain stories—either midrashim or the holiday stories themselves. For those chapters this section offers suggestions on how to present these stories as well as suggestions for discussions and reinforcing activities.

Teaching the Text

This section comments on individual sections of the text and offers ways of enhancing them. The headings here refer to the headings or lines from the student's text.

Suggested Activities

The textbook contains exercises designed to enhance comprehension, extend thinking, and promote discussion; use those activities in class as independent work or as small group exercises. This section of the Guide offers additional activities to integrate into your lesson. Some take a few minutes to complete, others require more in-depth consideration and advance planning. Art, drama, music, social action, and community projects all help to make learning more effective.

SPECIAL NOTE: Many of the activities in this section refer to page numbers from the book *Integrating Arts and Crafts in the Jewish School* by Carol Tauben and Edith Abrahams, published by Behrman House.

Teaching the Blessings

The holiday blessings have been provided throughout *My Jewish Year*. The blessings recited over Shabbat and holiday candles, wine, bread, the lulav and etrog, and the Hanukkah lights are a few examples. It is advisable to plan activities to help your students learn each one. In this way they will become familiar with the blessings and the formula for their construction.

The children will quickly notice the repetition of the first six words (*Baruch atah Adonai, eloheinu melech haolam . . .*). Many blessings continue with three more words (*asher kidshanu b'mitzvotav . . .*). You can point these out each time they appear.

If you know the tune for a blessing, always try to sing it to the class. Teaching a blessing as a song makes it easier to remember. Also, try to select one or two key Hebrew words to translate and teach as vocabulary. We all like to know the meaning of what we are saying. Here are some suggestions for blessing vocabulary to teach:

baruch	blessed
Adonai	God
melech	ruler
ner	candle
pri	fruit
lechem	bread

When you teach a new word from the blessings, you can have the children write it in Hebrew and English and then let them illustrate it. The words and illustrations can be put on index cards or flash cards. Each student can keep his or her own envelope of cards to study and to use for various games.

There are many games to play with Hebrew flash cards. One easy game is Memory. Place two sets of cards face down in rows. Have the children try to find the pairs. When a pair is found, the child must read the Hebrew word and tell its meaning in order to keep the pair. The person with the most cards at the end of the game is the winner. Another game is Pictionary. A child illustrates one of the words from the cards on the chalkboard. The others must find their corresponding card, hold it up, and name it.

When teaching a blessing, always try to have the class perform the actual act that the blessing intends. For example, if you are learning Hamotzi, have some bread on hand to eat after the blessing is recited. If you are learning to recite the lulav blessing, try to have a lulav available, and give each child the opportunity to shake it.

Remember, repetition is the most helpful tool. Review the blessings whenever you can. It will take only a minute or two. Encourage the children to recite the blessings at home with their family. As reinforcement, the blessings can be sent home as a part of the Family Education aspect of this program.

FAMILY EDUCATION COMPONENT

Educators today recognize the importance of involving the whole family in the education of the child. Doing so is particularly important when it comes to religious education.

The Family Education Experiences section at the end of this Guide offers programming suggestions for you and your community. Included are a variety of worksheets to send home. They will help families celebrate Jewishly. This section is an important one for you to consider when planning your lessons.

Each class's progression through the holiday materials presented in *My Jewish Year* will vary from school to school. Also, although a holiday falls on the same date every year according to the lunar Jewish calendar, this date will vary from year to year on the secular solar calendar. We've all heard: "Rosh Hashanah is late this year" or "Passover is coming early." Therefore, while the holidays in *My Jewish Year* are presented in the order of their celebration, children may actually be studying about a holiday well before or after its celebration (this is particularly true of the autumn holidays, which come in rapid succession at the beginning of the school year).

To empower the families of your children, it is most effective to plan Family Education holiday experiences a week or two *before* the actual celebration. (They will serve either as a precursor to what the children will be learning in school, or as a review of materials already studied.)

A wide variety of programming suggestions and parent/child worksheets is included in the Family Education section at the end of this Guide. Please feel free to select and duplicate the ones you find most appropriate.

ROSH HASHANAH

(Text pages 6–19)

Important Concepts

1. Rosh Hashanah marks the "birthday of the world" and a time of new beginnings for the Jewish people.

2. On Rosh Hashanah we evaluate our past behavior and pray that the new year will be a good one.

3. We celebrate Rosh Hashanah at home with a holiday meal, the lighting of candles, and blessings. We also send New Year's greeting cards.

4. We celebrate Rosh Hashanah in the synagogue with prayers, and we listen to the sound of the shofar.

5. We symbolically throw away our sins by performing the ritual of Tashlich.

Vocabulary

Rosh Hashanah The Hebrew word *rosh* means "head," and the word *shanah* means "year."

Shanah Tovah On Rosh Hashanah we wish everyone a good year with these words (the Hebrew word *tovah* means "good").

Sheheheyanu This blessing is said when we do something for the first time. Its recitation is therefore quite appropriate on the first evening of the New Year. The root of the word is *chai*, meaning "life."

Shofar A ram's horn.

Tashlich The root of this word is *shalach*, meaning "send away." See the Background Information for a further explanation.

Tishre The first month of the Jewish year. It is referred to in the Torah as the seventh month because Nisan (the month in which Passover is celebrated) was then considered the first month.

Yom Hadin "Day of Judgment," another name for Rosh Hashanah. *Yom* means "day," and *din* is the word for "judgment." The Hebrew name Dina comes from this root.

Yom Hazikaron "Day of Remembrance," another name for Rosh Hashanah. *Yom* means "day," and *zikaron* means "remembering." Yizkor, the service we recite to remember those who have died, comes from the same root.

Yom Teruah "Day of the Sounding of the Shofar." *Teruah* is the name of one of the three musical patterns blown on the shofar during the synagogue service. The sound is nine short blasts. The other two musical patterns are *tekiah*, a long blast to get our attention, and *shevarim*, three medium blasts, each consisting of two notes an interval of a musical fourth apart.

Background for the Teacher

A Personal Experience

Our family recently rented the video *Defending Your Life,* a movie in which a young man meets an untimely death in a car accident and finds himself in Judgment City, the place where all souls are asked to defend their lives before "moving on." The souls are shown scenes from their lives on earth and are then asked to defend their actions according to how well they dealt with fear. According to the movie, a person who responds to life with fear and caution doesn't progress to better things. Conversely, a person who shows courage is considered worthy of greater heights. This was all well and good, and mildly entertaining, but when the movie was over my children were somewhat confused.

"What was that stuff about fear?" my eight-year-old asked. "Doesn't God judge us by the things we *do*, like helping other people?" My husband smiled. Here was our daughter correcting Hollywood on a basic Jewish concept, making the assumption that the Jewish idea of being judged by our deeds is something everyone should take for granted. Hollywood might not get it, but we were glad that she did.

Rosh Hashanah, the head of the year, is one of the times when we make the effort to meditate on the theme of judgment. Our deeds of the past year loom before us and our hopes for the future develop. It is a day of rebirth and renewal, for ourselves and for the world. It is a day when we honor God in prayer and song and we rediscover our relationship with the Divine. These three themes, renewal, judgment, and the recognition of God's dominion, dominate the day. We live them in our preparations for the holiday, and in our celebration of it.

A Historical Perspective

Rosh Hashanah is first mentioned in the Torah when the book of Leviticus proclaims, "In the seventh month, in the first day of the month, there shall be a solemn rest for you, a sacred convocation commemorated with the blast of the ram's horn. You shall not work at any of your ordinary labor, and you shall bring a fire-offering to the Lord" (Lev. 23:24-25). In Biblical times, Tishre was considered the seventh month, since the first month was considered to be Nisan, the month in which Passover occurs. Spring, rather than autumn, was seen as the time of new beginnings.

After the destruction of the Temple in 586 B.C.E., our people, now relocated in Babylon, began to absorb some of the customs of their new neighbors. The Babylonians celebrated harvest time as the beginning of their year, and so the Jews followed suit, giving Rosh Hashanah greater significance. While the Babylonians celebrated the successful completion of their harvest and pledged renewed loyalty to the Babylonian throne, the Jews transformed the theme of their holiday into a renewal of their loyalty to God.

In about 485 B.C.E., when the Jews returned to the Land of Israel after the Babylonian exile, Nehemiah, the new governor, chose the first of Tishre as the date of a holy convocation to hear the Torah being read aloud. The people gathered at the Water Gate in Jerusalem to hear the Torah reading and the explanation of the text. People wept when they realized how far their lives had drifted from the Torah. But Ezra the Scribe and the Levites told them to celebrate, to feast and to share with those who had nothing. They reminded the people that this day was a holiday and that their rediscovery of Torah should be a time of joy. This special day was an opportunity to change one's life and to turn again toward Torah.

As the years progressed, the holiday of Rosh Hashanah developed, taking on new layers of meaning. Not only was it the day when we celebrated the recrowning of God as King, it also became the day of judgment, when we examined our lives and vowed to improve ourselves. During the Mishnaic period (first and second centuries C.E.), Rabbi Eliezer taught that the world was created during the month of Tishre, solidifying the theme of new beginnings.

The Talmud tractate *Rosh Hashanah* embellishes the motif of judgment as it tells of the three celestial books that are opened on Rosh Hashanah. One is for the completely righteous, one for the completely wicked, and the third for those in between. The evildoers are inscribed in the book of death, and the righteous in the book of life. Their fates are sealed immediately. The average people, however, have ten days—from Rosh Hashanah until Yom Kippur—to atone for their sins and make it into the book of life.

In the Synagogue

The liturgy for the holidays is unique enough to warrant its own special prayerbook called a Mahzor. You can familiarize your students with the Sheheheyanu blessing that we say the first evening we light the holiday candles, as well as a few of the basic prayers.

The prayer Avinu Malkenu appears at various times through the holiday services. It expresses the basic theme of *teshuvah*, returning to God. The special holiday Kiddush is sung, and many familiar prayers such as Shema and Barechu are sung with melodies that sound more contemplative than the melodies used during the rest of the year.

The Torah readings include the story of the binding of Isaac and the story of Sarah giving birth to Isaac after years of barrenness. These stories all revolve around themes of faith, human nature, and our relationship to God.

The Shofar

One of the most beautiful aspects of Rosh Hashanah is the sounding of the shofar. The ancient sound calls to that primal place in our souls, waking us up, commanding our attention. Saadia Gaon, a ninth-century teacher, listed ten reasons why we are commanded to blow the shofar. They can be summed up as follows:

1. The shofar calls us to change our ways.

2. The shofar heralds God's monarchy as trumpets herald a monarch.

3. The shofar was heard at Sinai as a war alarm at the destruction of the Temple, and it will be heard again on the great day of judgment when the Messiah comes.

Tashlich

Another event that occurs on Rosh Hashanah is Tashlich. From the root *shalach*, which means "send off," Tashlich is the symbolic act of casting off sin by throwing the crumbs from one's pockets into a moving body of water. Some say that the custom comes from the Prophet Micah, who speaks of God casting the sins of Israel into the depths of the sea (Micah 7:19). Some say we throw our sins into the sea because the fish who live there remind us of God—their eyes are always open, always watching.

Rosh Hashanah Customs

Other customs include eating round hallah and dipping apples in honey. It is also customary to send greeting cards to friends and family.

Rosh Hashanah is celebrated for two days, even in Israel. This custom originated in the days when fires on mountaintops and the sound of the shofar were the means by which the proper date of observance was signaled from one community to another. In order to ensure that everyone celebrated Rosh Hashanah at the correct time, an extra day was added for leeway. Some Reform communities celebrate the holiday for one day.

Introducing the Lesson

Engage the children in a discussion of what happens on their birthdays. Ask them to explain what they are celebrating and to list the various things that are necessary in order to celebrate a birthday properly. Write this list on the board.

Next introduce the concept of the world having a birthday. Explain that we have to make a party for the world and will need the same things that we need to celebrate our own birthday. On the chalkboard, list the items we need to celebrate our birthday. Next to each item list the comparable item for the world's birthday.

Example:

cake	hallah (round)
candles	holiday candles
singing "Happy Birthday"	singing our prayers
ice cream and candy	apples and honey
sending birthday cards	sending New Year cards

Finally, compare your students' age to the age of the world. Show the Hebrew year that is ending and the one that is beginning. Point out how the earth is becoming one year older, just as they do on their birthdays.

You might want to show some pictures of birthday parties to help stimulate the initial discussion.

Teaching the Text

Long, long ago . . . You can supplement this creation information by reading the story from the Torah or from one of the many picture books that recount it. Assign each child one day of creation. As you read the story, have them act out each day.

What Are You Thankful For? Ask the class what it means to thank God. How do we do this? (With prayer and blessings.) List some of the things the children are thankful for. Use the list to make a book, a bulletin board, a poster, etc.

A Day of Remembering Take this opportunity to review the new Jewish year. Teach the word *rosh*, meaning "head," and the word *yom*, meaning "day." Ask the students, "When does the month of Tishre occur?" (In the fall.) What are some other things that happen during Tishre? (Leaves change color, school starts, holidays are celebrated—Sukkot, Yom Kippur, Simhat Torah.)

Rosh Hashanah is a day of hope . . . List the things your students hope for. Let each child draw them, and make a mural from the drawings.

At Home Ask why we wear our best clothes on Rosh Hashanah. Practice the blessings. See the Introduction at the beginning of this guide for suggested activities around the blessings.

On the table is a loaf of hallah bread . . . Can you think of other reasons why the bread is round? (Life goes round like a circle, the earth is round.)

A Sweet Year Sample the foods and practice the proper blessings.

New Year Cards Learn to write *Shanah Tovah* in Hebrew. Make New Year cards. Discuss to whom you would send them and why.

In the Synagogue Visit the sanctuary to see the Torah. Let the children hold and touch the Torah, always being careful to preserve an air of holiness. Explain that the *rimonim* and *keter* have bells so that the Torah makes noise as it is carried through the sanctuary.

This makes the listeners look up and pay attention. Explain the parts of a Torah and how it is made. (You can save this activity for Simhat Torah if you wish.)

The Shofar Ask the students how people were able to communicate with others far away before there were telephones. Explain that the shofar was used for this purpose. Let the children try blowing a shofar. Invite someone to class to perform the shofar calls.

Tashlich Discuss where you could do Tashlich in your community. Plan to do it together.

Suggested Activities

1. **Make a creation book.** Staple seven pages together to form a book and have the children illustrate one day of creation on each page. Read Genesis, Chapter 1, to pick out the order of events.

2. **Make a birthday book for the world.** Each page can be a scene of a beautiful place on earth. These can be freehand illustrations or pictures cut from magazines. Children can include their hopes and wishes as well as the things they are thankful for.

3. **Do a fall leaf project.** On a white sheet of paper create a colorful abstract design. Use fall colors and cover the whole sheet. Next, take a black sheet of paper the same size and cut designs in it in the shapes of various leaves. Place the black page over the white one, letting the color show through.

4. **Make New Years cards.** Draw a honey pot on the cover of a New Year card. Cut an apple in half, dip it in paint or ink, and use it to print apple shapes around the honey pot. Write *Shanah Tovah* inside the card. Try to have the students write it in Hebrew.

5. **Eat hallah, apples, and honey and practice the proper blessings.**

6. **Learn to bake a round hallah.** At home, prepare enough dough for all the children. A lump the size of a large fist should be enough for each student. Frozen white bread dough that is all vegetarian can be purchased at many supermarkets if you need to save

time. The children can form the hallah in class. After you bake the hallah, you can practice reciting the blessing over the bread before you eat it.

7. **Make a shofar out of paper towel rolls.** See *Integrating Arts and Crafts in the Jewish School*, pages 68–70.

8. **Learn to blow the shofar.** Have your cantor or other knowledgeable person teach the calls.

9. **Read the following story to the class.** There is a well-known Hasidic tale for Rosh Hashanah about a boy who thinks he is unable to pray but discovers that God hears his earnest prayers even though they are offered in an unorthodox fashion. The source is *Kehal Hasidim Hehadash*, Lvov, 1906. It is retold in many other places, with some variation. There are three versions of it in *Jewish Folktales* by Pinhas Sadeh (New York: Doubleday, 1989), pages 394, 395, 396.

FAMILY EDUCATION IDEAS ARE LOCATED AT THE END OF THIS GUIDE

YOM KIPPUR

(Text pages 20-33)

Important Concepts

1. During the ten days between Rosh Hashanah and Yom Kippur (known as the Ten Days of Repentance), we examine our lives, and we think of times during the past year when we have "missed the mark." We apologize to those we have hurt.

2. On Yom Kippur we ask God to forgive us for the wrong things we have done. This practice is called *teshuvah*, or repentance. Doing *teshuvah* helps us to feel closer to God.

3. We light yahrzeit candles and participate in the Yizkor service to remember relatives and friends who have died.

4. Adults fast on Yom Kippur. It is a way for them to show God how sorry they are, and it helps them to think about how to become better people in the year ahead.

5. There are many special prayers recited on Yom Kippur. These include Kol Nidre and Al Het.

6. Observing Yom Kippur helps us to reflect on ways to make our world a better place. This act of repairing the world is called *tikkun olam*.

Vocabulary

Al Het A communal confession. The Hebrew word *het* means sin, or more literally, "missing the mark." This prayer is a list of sins recited in the first person plural.

Aseret Y'mei Teshuvah The ten days between Rosh Hashanah and Yom Kippur. It is traditional during this time to reflect on our deeds, apologize to those we have harmed, and give extra tzedakah.

Day of Atonement The English name for the holiday Yom Kippur.

Fasting On Yom Kippur a 25-hour fast is observed during which we neither eat nor drink.

Het The Hebrew word for "sin," which means "to miss the mark."

Kol Nidre The prayer sung on erev Yom Kippur that releases us from vows made to God which we were unable to keep. See the Background Information section for some history concerning this prayer.

Tekiah Gedolah A long, loud blast of the shofar that ends the Ne'ilah service, the concluding service on Yom Kippur. *Gedolah* means "large" in Hebrew.

Teshuvah Repentance. The word literally means "returning" in Hebrew.

Tzedakah From the Hebrew root *tzedek*, meaning righteous. Tzedakah refers to doing the right and fair thing. It can take many forms, not just monetary gifts.

Yahrzeit Candle The candle we light to remember someone who is no longer alive. The Yiddish word *yahrzeit* can also refer to the Hebrew anniversary of that person's death.

Yizkor A service on Yom Kippur, Sukkot, Passover, and Shavuot during which we remember people who have died. The Kaddish prayer is recited at this time.

Background Information

General Background

Yom Kippur is the day on which God and the Jewish people stand face to face. We stand confronted by our errors, our shortcomings, and our sorrows, and we ask God for understanding and forgiveness. We examine our relationships with others and with God, and we vow to improve our behavior. In exchange, God accepts our atonement, and our misdeeds are forgiven.

According to the *aggadah* (the non-legal portion of the Oral Torah), several pivotal events in our history took place on Yom Kippur. Abraham is said to have been circumcised on that day, Moses is said to have received the second Tablets of the Law, and Isaac was tied to the altar on Mount Moriah.

A Historical Perspective

The special significance of Yom Kippur is described in the book of Leviticus. "Mark, the tenth day of the seventh month is the day of atonement. There shall be a holy convocation onto you, and you shall afflict your souls. You shall bring an offering made by fire onto the Lord. And you shall do no manner of work on that same day, for it is a day of atonement, to make atonement for you before the Lord your God" (Lev. 23:27-28).

In the days of the Temple, on the tenth of Tishre the high priest conducted special sacrifices to cleanse the Temple shrine and the people. Three animals were picked by lot to sacrifice for three separate confessions. A bull and a goat were sacrificed to rid the Temple of any defilement that might have been caused by the misdeeds of the priests. A third goat, the goat marked for "Azazel" (the evil one), was sacrificed in a different manner. The priest would first lay his hands upon the goat's head and confess the sins of the people, thereby placing all the errors of the Israelites on the animal's head. The goat was then chased off a cliff in the wilderness. This event is the origin of the English word "scapegoat."

The priest made three confessions, one over each animal. As each confession reached a peak, the priest would recite the holy name of God aloud, and then the people would prostrate themselves and recite the second line of the Shema (*Baruch Shem k'vod malchuto l'olam va-ed*). Each time, the priest would enter the Holy of Holies, the innermost room of the Temple where God's Presence was said to be most strongly felt. The mood was solemn. Then after the goat was sacrificed, the mood shifted to joy. Sin had been removed from the midst of the people, and it was now time to celebrate. When the Temple was destroyed in 70 C.E. the customs of sacrifice and the scapegoat disappeared, and the rituals of Yom Kippur took on a new shape. The command to afflict one's soul was defined in a different manner. One was now expected to refrain from food, drink, washing, sexual intercourse, and the wearing of leather shoes. Sacrifice was replaced by a full 25 hours of prayer, which was once described by the first-century Jewish philosopher Philo of Alexandria as "one long blessing before an enormous meal."

Kol Nidre

The evening service is dominated by the dramatic prayer Kol Nidre. Three members representing a heavenly court stand before the rest of the congregation. The Kol Nidre prayer is chanted three times, the melody beautiful and haunting. The words declare that the court of justice will permit all sinners to pray in each other's presence. All vows and oaths made to God in the previous year that the sinner was unable to fulfill are to be null and void.

Kol Nidre is a strange and confusing prayer, one that makes more sense when seen in the context of the time in which it was written. During the period of the Spanish inquisition, many Spanish Jews saved their lives by taking public oaths in order to become publicly Christian. They remained Jews, however, worshipping in secret on Rosh Hashanah, Yom Kippur, and other holidays. These Jews needed a way to absolve themselves from these public oaths that they never meant to keep.

The Yom Kippur Service

The Yom Kippur morning service contains a prayer, the Vidui, in which our misdeeds are listed in alphabetical order. We recite the whole list, even though as individuals we could not have possibly committed them all. The prayer Al Het is also recited by everyone, in the first person plural. "We have sinned" rather than "I have sinned" is the message, for we stand as a community on this day, praying for others as well as ourselves, reminding ourselves that it is the group that makes us strong.

An interesting aspect of the Yom Kippur service is that the second line of the Shema (*Baruch Shem K'vod malchuto l'olam va-ed*) is recited aloud. It is a dramatic moment, for in most Conservative and Orthodox synagogues that line is usually recited quietly during the rest of the year. The reciting of this line is a symbol reminding us of the sacrificial ritual of the Second Temple period, when this phrase was chanted by the whole community before the high priest.

The day also contains a special service called Yizkor, in which we remember our friends and relatives who have died. The Kaddish prayer is said at this time as well as El Malei Rahamim.

In terms of teaching children, the most interesting reading for the holiday is the haftarah from the book of Jonah. This is traditionally heard during the Mincha service on Yom Kippur afternoon. Everyone in this story is involved with repentance: Jonah, the people of Ninevah, and God. You may want to read this story aloud and discuss it with your class.

The day concludes with a service called Ne'ilat Hash'arim, literally "the closing of the gates." We refer to it as Ne'ilah for short. We have prayed all day. We are tired and hungry, and the sun is setting. We pray fervently that our prayers have been sufficiently honest. We hope that they will lend us passage through the heavenly gates so that our names will be sealed into the Book of Life. The long blast of the shofar signals the end of the day, and we joyfully sing, "Next Year in Jerusalem."

Rituals

Ten days are set aside between Rosh Hashanah and Yom Kippur. Known as the Ten Days of Repentance, they give us time to make restitution to those whom we feel we have harmed, and to speak honestly with God. It is also customary to give special tzedakah during these days and to study the Prophets and the later books of the Bible. The special Shabbat that occurs during this week is known as *Shabbat Teshuvah*.

It is customary on the day before Yom Kippur to eat and drink well, especially in the late afternoon before the start of the holiday. Traditional Jews visit the mikveh, the ritual bath, and then dress in clean white clothing. Some say this represents purity; others say it enables us to resemble the angels. Some people wear a *kittel*, a special white tunic that is worn on special occasions: Yom Kippur, Passover, one's wedding, and as a shroud upon one's death. Cloth shoes are worn instead of leather.

The late afternoon meal is eaten without reciting the Kiddush. Holiday candles, as well as a Yizkor candle, are lit after the meal. This candle lighting signals that the holiday has begun.

Many prefer to stay in synagogue all day so that concentration is not broken and the temptations of home are avoided. Children should, of course, eat their meals, but they might give up something for the day, such as snacks or perhaps breakfast.

After the sounding of the shofar comes the break-the-fast meal. This is a particularly festive time and is much more pleasant when enjoyed in groups. Some synagogues serve a break-the-fast meal for its members; some Jews gather at the homes of friends. Traditional foods for this meal are kugels, lox and bagels, juices, salads. No one wants to eat anything too heavy after a day of fasting.

There is a tradition of going home from Ne'ilah and hammering the first nail into the Sukkah. It is a symbolic way of looking forward to the festival that begins only four days later. The somber day of prayer is over, and the harvest celebration is about to begin.

Introducing the Lesson

The word for "sin" in Hebrew is *het*, but *het* for a Jew does not carry the same connotations as the word sin does in English. While sin calls to mind evil deeds, *het* means simply "missing the mark," trying to do the right thing but not quite succeeding. This Jewish notion of sin assumes that we are good souls who sometimes get sidetracked, who sometimes fail in our mission. It is difficult to separate the severe English sense of the word from the Jewish sense, and therefore it is better for us to say that we are looking for ways in which we have "missed the mark" rather than the ways we have sinned. The following exercise may illustrate the point and also serve as an appropriate way to introduce this chapter.

Have the children play some sort of target game. You can draw a big target on the chalkboard and have each child, one at a time, attempt to throw an eraser at the bull's-eye. You can also play trash can basketball or bean bag throw. Don't make it easy. Remember, you want most of the children to miss. Instruct them to try very hard to hit the mark. Give everyone a turn and then discuss the results.

Ask them if they were all perfect. When they respond "no," ask if that means they weren't trying. Make the connection to real life. Explain that sometimes we "miss the mark" in life, even when we are trying our hardest. We want to be perfect, but we can't always be so. Explain that Yom Kippur is a chance to work with God to improve our performance in life and to erase the bad times when we have missed.

Teaching the Text

We always try to do the right thing . . . The Jewish concept of sin is best described as "missing the mark." Relate this paragraph to the exercise from the section Introducing the Lesson. List various ways in which we "miss the mark." Include things we forget to do or avoid doing, as well as bad things we have actually done.

After we hurt someone it can be hard to say "I'm sorry" . . . Have the class discuss the many ways to say that one is sorry: words, gifts, acts of kindness, repairing broken items, etc.

The Ten Days of Repentance Be sure to define forgiveness. Explain how the Hebrew word for repentance is *teshuvah*, which literally means "returning." Ask the students how walking away from something or someone and them returning to that person or to God can mean the same thing as repentance. List the different ways people can repent. Another traditional thing to do during these days is to give tzedakah. The class can take on a tzedakah project at this time.

The Day of Atonement Ask the class what we do when we want to get close to people. Compare these with the things we do to get close to God.

At Home Discuss ways we remember people who are no longer alive. (Naming people and places after them, planting trees in Israel, giving money in their memory, writing books about them, etc.)

Fasting Discuss how children can fast in a manner suitable to their young age (not eat snacks or junk food, etc.). Discuss why we fast (as a personal punishment, to help us think about our deeds, to help us understand the problems of those who don't have enough to eat). Talk about what it's like for children who don't have enough to eat every day.

Kol Nidre Ask your students to list the promises that they made but were not able to keep, or perhaps promises their parents made but were not able to keep. Point out how this can happen very easily, even when we don't want it to. Explain a bit of the history of Kol Nidre. Pretend that the class is a group of Spanish Jews and it is Yom Kippur. Have them prepare a prayer (like Kol Nidre) of their own.

Al Het Discuss the importance of saying our prayers using the word "we." Why is it different from saying "I"? Why do we say this prayer out loud? Why do some people tap their chests with their fists?

Breaking the Fast Discuss how it feels to pray all day. Why do you think people do that? Explain how Yom Kippur ends, with the imagery of *Ne'ilah* (the closing of the gates) and the final blowing of the shofar. You might want to show a shofar again at this point and have someone demonstrate the *tekiah gedolah*. Ask the class why they think the holiday ends with a blast of the shofar.

Making the World a Better Place Discuss what it feels like to be clean. Ask them how they feel after they take a long, warm bath. This is the feeling we get at the end of Yom Kippur. Think of things your class or school can do to repair the world. Perhaps the children are already doing some of them.

Suggested Activities

1. **Draw a time line of ten boxes to represent the ten days between Rosh Hashanah and Yom Kippur.** Make them large enough to write within each box. Have the children talk about the different ways they can do teshuvah during these days. Begin the line with a symbol of Rosh Hashanah, such as a round hallah or a shofar. End the line with a symbol of Yom Kippur, such as a yahrzeit candle.

2. **Make a large mural depicting the ways people can do teshuvah.**

3. **Have the class write an original prayer on the theme of teshuvah.** It can have one entry for each letter of the alphabet like the Vidui prayer.
(e.g., We will: Always listen to our parents
                     Be more helpful
                     Clean our rooms, etc.)

4. **See if your religious school can sponsor a tzedakah fair during the ten days of repentance as a part of the school's activities.** The staff can gather information on a variety of charities, many of which should be Jewish ones, and then make a booth for each charity. As families walk around, each booth should compete for your tzedakah coins by explaining its cause.

5. **Lead a discussion of what it is like not to have enough to eat.** Help the class decide to participate in a tzedakah project having to do with hunger. They can bring in cans of food for the local food bank or give a small donation to one of the many hunger relief organizations.

6. **Listen to the Kol Nidre prayer.** Discuss its meaning and the ways in which the tune enhances the meaning.

7. **Learn to sing Avinu Malkenu.** You can also learn to sing the Shema, Barechu, and Mi Chamocha.

8. **Read the stories, "I'm Sorry" and "The Announcing Tool" from** *The World of The High Holidays,* **edited by Rabbi Jack Reimer (Bernie Books).**

9. **Make a shofar or a bookmark.** See *Integrating Arts and Crafts in the Jewish School,* pages 68-71.

10. **Read the story of Jonah and discuss its relation to the themes of Yom Kippur.**

FAMILY EDUCATION IDEAS ARE LOCATED AT THE END OF THIS GUIDE

SUKKOT

(Text pages 34-45)

Important Concepts

1. On Sukkot we thank God for the food that we harvest in the fall.

2. We celebrate Sukkot by building a sukkah, a "booth."

3. The sukkah reminds us of the booths that the farmers slept in during harvest time in ancient Israel. They also remind us of the temporary structures used by the Jews who wandered in the wilderness on the way to the Land of Israel.

4. Sukkot is one of the three Pilgrimage Festivals described in the Torah. During these holidays, Jews were expected to travel to Jerusalem to give thanks in the Holy Temple.

5. Sukkot lasts for seven days.

6. We wave the lulav and the etrog. When we point the lulav and etrog in every direction, we are showing that God is everywhere.

7. On Sukkot we say special prayers of thanksgiving called Hallel.

Vocabulary

Etrog The etrog is known as a citron in English. It is a yellow, lemon-like fruit.

Hachnasat Orhim This means literally "Allowing guests to enter." Hachnasat Orhim is one of the mitzvot we can fulfill during the holidays; a holiday table seems lacking without invited guests.

Hag Samayah The Hebrew words for "happy holiday," this is the customary greeting to say on Sukkot.

Hallel These prayers of thanks are Psalms 113-118. They all have traditional melodies.

Lulav The combination of palm, myrtle, and willow that we hold and wave on Sukkot.

Shemini Atzeret The day at the end of Sukkot when we pray for rain. It is also customary to say Yizkor (a memorial service) on that day.

Sukkah A temporary structure we build to remind us of the days when our ancestors lived in them. See the Background Information for specific construction rules.

Z'man Simhataynu Simha means "joy." *Z'man* means "time." The phrase literally means "Time to be happy." The Torah refers to Sukkot as the "Season of our Joy."

Background Information

A Personal Experience

Building the sukkah each year is my husband's job. He loves tools and wood and sawdust but has little opportunity during the year to make the cabinets and bookcases he enjoys building. So, when fall arrives, he is glad to take out his power tools and build our sukkah.

Each year our sukkah gets bigger and better. From the small urban plywood one we began with fifteen years ago, we have moved on to a paneled, latticework, pre-fab sukkah that folds and stores for the winter.

When the sukkah is being built, everyone gets into the act. The children use the tools, hammering their fingers (and sometimes actually helping). My Catholic neighbor gets his truck for the trip to the lumber yard. (We have never had shy neighbors. Ever since the year one of them asked if we were building a new garage, they have come by to help, even going so far as to show off the finished product to their priests!) The walls are put together on the ground. We all lift and carry, hammer and trim the walls until they stand alone. After a snack, we trim the pines for the *s'chach* on the roof, and then we decorate.

This is when my daughter appears. Knowing full well that the heavy manual labor is done, she comes out prepared to hang her artistic creations as high as we will allow her to climb on the ladder. Over the years we have tried every decoration in the book, but unfortunately, unlike in the land of Israel, we know we will get rain sometime during the seven-day holiday; since most decorations are paper, we hang them and try not to think about what will happen. For this reason I like to use Indian corn and fruits and vegetables sprayed with shellac. (Spraying the fruit with shellac was a tip from an old friend who took pity on us one year as we were attacked by a large swarm of sukkah bees.) We hang flowers, New Year's cards, origami creations, just about anything. Our sukkah is always colorful and bright with the fragrant smell of pine, and a pumpkin on the table.

Why Build a Sukkah?

I try to tell the parents of my students, "Building a sukkah is the Jewish Christmas tree experience." What do I mean by that?

When your child comes home in December and says, "Why can't we have a Christmas tree? They smell so good and they're so nice to decorate," what can you say?

"Well," you reply, "a Christmas tree is a Christian symbol. We don't believe in what it represents."

That's true, of course, but the child is also right. Why should he or she be deprived of such a lovely experience?

So it is important to tell a child that a sukkah is a Jewish symbol. It offers a sensory experience equivalent to a Christmas tree, and it is a part of *our* holiday observance: There's a nip in the air. There's the smell of pine and apples. The spiny lulav and the fragrant etrog are in your hands. It's a quiet morning. No one else is out. You shake the lulav as was done in the ancient Temple courtyard, and you feel timeless in your own backyard. Before getting ready for work, you sit for a moment among the paper chains the children have made. You could sit there forever. Sitting in a sukkah can make all things feel right.

Creating a sukkah is the same sort of communal experience as decorating a tree, so why don't more people take advantage of that? Rather than dwelling on the things we don't do, we should simply make sure to do the things we are supposed to do. Why not build a sukkah?

Historical Background

Sukkot, also known as the "Feast of Booths," is mentioned several times in the Torah. Leviticus 23:39-43 tells us:

> On the fifteenth day of the seventh month, when you have gathered in the
> fruits of the land, you shall keep the feast of the Lord seven days; on the
> first day shall be a solemn rest, and on the eighth day shall be a solemn
> rest. On the first day you shall take the fruit of goodly trees, branches of
> palm trees, and boughs of thick trees, and willows of the brook, and you
> shall rejoice before your God seven days. And you shall keep it a feast onto
> your God seven days in the year; it is a statute forever in your generations;
> you shall keep it in the seventh month. You shall dwell in booths seven

days; all that are home born in Israel shall dwell in booths; that your generation might know that I made the children of Israel to dwell in booths when I brought them out of the land of Egypt. I am the Lord your God.

Despite the commandment to dwell in booths, Nehemiah, who returned to Jerusalem after the Babylonian exile, reports that from the time of Joshua until his own time this was not the practice (Neh. 8:17). The prophet says that people regularly began to build booths and celebrate Sukkot only in his own day. As the Second Temple was completed, the tradition of building sukkot and bringing lulav and etrog ("the fruit of goodly trees") to the Temple for special rituals became quite popular. People would bring their own and wave it east, south, west, and north in an elaborate, joyous ceremony. Willow branches were placed around the altar, and to the sound of the shofar the priest would march around the altar, lulav in hand, calling, "Save us now, we beseech thee, O Lord! Send now prosperity."

A dramatic part of the ritual, not mentioned in the Torah itself, was the water pouring ceremony. Great fires were lit in the Temple courtyard. Huge golden candlesticks burned as flutes, harps, and trumpets played, and the people danced. The event inspired the Mishnah comment: "He that has never seen the joy of the *Beth HaShoevah* has never in his life seen joy."

During Temple times, music, dancing, bonfires, and fervent prayer were all a part of the thanks that were offered for the harvest. Jerusalem became crowded with worshippers, for Sukkot is one of the three Pilgrimage Festivals on which Jews traveled to Jerusalem with their offerings. People climbed the hills to the Holy City from all the outlying areas, bringing with them bulls, rams, and lambs for the sacrifices. The streets became crowded as families camped out in sukkot with their livestock. It was a time to visit with friends and family who lived in other regions, to feast and to celebrate.

With the destruction of the Temple in 70 C.E., the sacrifices, the pilgrimage, and the water pouring ceremony ceased to exist. We were transplanted to faraway places, left to rework the old customs into new forms. Rabbi Johanan ben Zakkai, a scholar of that period, helped to give the holiday the new direction it needed. He ordained that wherever Jews might live they were to take the four species in hand to remember the Temple. They were to chant Hallel (Psalms 113-118) and build sukkot. Today these customs remain with us.

How to Build a Sukkah

We are instructed to build a sukkah during the four days between Yom Kippur and the start of Sukkot. The sukkah can be no more than ten yards high but no less than ten handbreadths (so that there is room to raise the lulav over one's head). It must have at least three walls, and the roof must be thatched so that there is more shade than sun. Yet it should not be so thickly thatched that the rain cannot penetrate. The structure must feel temporary. The roof covering is called *s'chach*. Rushes, pine branches, or corn husks can be used as long as they come from the soil. The sukkah must sit out in the open, not under a tree or roof, and it should be "adorned" (decorated).

The Lulav and the Etrog

The ritual lulav and etrog are made up of what we call "the four species" or the *arba'ah minim*. Three myrtle twigs and two willow branches are bound together with one stiff palm branch. The etrog, or citron, is a citrus fruit grown in Israel. It is larger than a lemon, with a distinctive aroma. Its small stem is called the *pitom*. The etrog's pitom must be intact and the fruit itself must be without blemish to be acceptable for ritual use. Sets of lulav and etrog can be purchased from Jewish bookstores or synagogues as the holiday approaches.

There are several midrashim that attempt to explain the selection of these four species—myrtle, willow, palm, and etrog—to represent the Sukkot harvest. One says that they represent the four letters of God's name. Another says they represent four different kinds of Jews: the etrog is the Torah scholar who does good deeds; the palm, the scholar who does not act; the myrtle, the doer of good deeds who does not study; and the willow, the one that does neither. The four species have also been compared to four parts of the human body: the etrog as the heart, the palm as the spine, the myrtle as the eye, and the willow as the mouth.

How We Celebrate

Sukkot begins on the fifteenth of Tishre. There is a full moon on this night. During the first two days of Sukkot (although only the first day in Israel and among Reform Jews) we are to refrain from work. Candles are lit in the evening, and Kiddush and the Hamotzi (the blessing over bread) are recited. If weather permits (the Talmud states that we do not have to endure hardship when sitting in the sukkah), dinner is served in the sukkah.

It is said that Rabbi Isaac Luria, the sixteenth-century mystic of Safed, invited each of the seven biblical shepherds into his sukkah, one each night. These men were

Abraham, Isaac, Jacob, Joseph, Moses, Aaron, and David. Our family enjoys this ritual at home, adding biblical women to the list of guests. This custom is known as *ushpizin*.

When you eat in a sukkah there is an extra blessing to be said: *Baruch atah Adonai, eloheinu melech haolam, asher kidshanu b'mitzvotav v'tzivanu leyshev basukkah.* "Blessed are You, Adonai our God, who makes us holy through your commandments and commands us to sit in the sukkah." On the first night we add the Sheheheyanu blessing.

The morning service is reminiscent of Temple days. In many synagogues congregants bring their own lulavim to the service. The lulav is carried in a parade around the bimah just as the priest marched around the altar years ago. There is an addition to the Amidah (the silent devotion), and Hallel is recited.

At the synagogue, everyone has a chance to wave the lulav. To do this, hold the lulav in your right hand with the myrtle on the right and the willow on the left, and hold the etrog in your left hand with the pitom facing down. Hold the hands close together and say the blessing. On the first day of Sukkot add the Sheheheyanu. Then, as you hold the four species together, turn the etrog so the pitom is on top. Face east and shake the lulav and etrog in six directions: first front, then to the right, then over the shoulder, next to your left, then to the sky, and finally to the ground.

The seventh day of Sukkot is known as *Hoshanah Rabbah*. This is the time when the priests marched around the altar seven times, waving the lulav and beating its leaves into the ground. We preserve this custom today, marking the end of the ritual life of the lulav. Some people save the etrog to make jelly or spice for the Havdalah box. The palm can be saved for Passover to sweep crumbs of hametz, and some people save the willow to heat the Pesah oven. It's nice to think of ways to tie the holidays together.

The Torah readings for Sukkot are from the book Leviticus. These readings describe the ritual obligations for the holiday. The haftarah portion contains Solomon's dedication of the First Temple, which occurred the week before Sukkot.

The eighth day of Sukkot is known as Shemini Atzeret. This holiday includes holiday candles, Kiddush, Hallel, and the Yizkor service, in which we remember those who have passed away. Special prayers for rain are added on this day, and we continue to say them until Passover. Reform Jews combine Shemini Atzeret with the celebration of Simhat Torah.

The Talmud tells us during the week of Sukkot the sukkah should be our primary abode. Offering hospitality in our sukkah is important, and tzedakah should be given. To whatever degree we manage to fulfill these obligations, we can all celebrate this special week by renewing the ties to our past, rejoicing in who we are, and considering who we can be.

Introducing the Lesson

First, ask the class to define the word "harvest." Ask them, "When does harvest occur? What do we do? What sort of foods do we harvest?" Pictures of farms or people picking fruit in an orchard might enhance the discussion.

Next, ask the class if we have an American holiday to celebrate the harvest. They will probably answer Thanksgiving. Discuss why having a good harvest is so important and worthy of celebration.

Tell the class that Jewish people really have two Thanksgivings. The Jewish harvest celebration is known as Sukkot, and it is described in the Torah. You might want to list the various ways we celebrate each holiday and compare the lists.

Thanksgiving	**Sukkot**
We eat turkey and other harvest foods.	We build a Sukkah.
We give thanks to God.	We wave the lulav and etrog.
Families and friends get together.	We eat harvest foods.
We learn about our American history.	We eat and sleep in our sukkah.
	We give thanks to God (Hallel).
	Families and friends get together.
	We learn about our Jewish past.

Explain to the children that the Pilgrims were very religious people. They had read about Sukkot in the Bible, and they knew that the Jewish people had a special harvest holiday. When it came time for the Pilgrims' first harvest in the New World, they wanted to have a Sukkot, too. That is how they created the first Thanksgiving. So we should be proud to know that the concept of the Thanksgiving holiday grew out of the holiday of Sukkot.

Finally, point out to the class that while celebrating Thanksgiving is relatively simple, there are many things one needs to know in order to enjoy Sukkot, and that the class is going to learn all about them.

Teaching the Text

When you eat a peanut butter and jelly sandwich . . . Ask the children to name other food we harvest in the fall. Ask them if they can name different foods that might be harvested in Israel.

How Sukkot Got Its Name Ask the children how the harvest is different today than in biblical times. Would we still need to live in booths? Why do we live in booths during this holiday? Name the other two pilgrimage festivals (Passover and Shavuot). What sort of gifts do we give God now that we don't bring sheep and goats to the Temple? (Prayers and deeds.)

Wandering in the Desert What other holiday reminds us of wandering in the desert? (Passover.)

How We Build a Sukkah Make a list or booklet of the rules for sukkah building. Have the children talk about building a sukkah at home or helping at the synagogue. Make some decorations in class.

What We Do in the Sukkah Practice the blessing. Talk about what it might be like to sleep in a sukkah all night.

Welcoming Guests Discuss the characters that Rabbi Isaac Luria invited to his sukkah, listed earlier in the "How We Celebrate" section. Ask the children what they can remember about each one. Whom would they like to invite to their own sukkah?

The Lulav and the Etrog Try to have a lulav and etrog in class. Let your students smell the etrog and shake the lulav in the six directions. Ask the children if they can create other midrashim about the meaning of the four species.

Giving to Others Ask your class why it is necessary in Israel to pray for rain.

Books on Sukkot

    1. *Molly's Pilgrim* by Barbara Cohen (New York: Lothrop, Lee and Sheperd, 1983) makes the connection between Thanksgiving and Sukkot.

2. *The House on the Roof* by David Adler (KarBen Copies, 1976) describes how an old man builds a sukkah on his roof despite his landlady's objections.

3. *The Big Sukkah* by Penninah Schram (KarBen Copies, 1986) deals with the mitzvah of hospitality.

4. "The Etrog" from *Holiday Tales of Sholom Aleichem*, edited by Aliza Shevrin (Athenium, 1979) is about a boy who breaks the pitom of his father's valuable etrog, and how he comes to accept responsibility for this act.

Suggested Activities

1. **Make sukkah decorations.** Some suggestions for decorations are origami, fusion beads, cranberry-popcorn chains, small decorated baskets, papier-mache fruit (page 79 in *Integrating Arts And Crafts in the Jewish School*), paper chains, paper flowers, etc.

2. **Make a shoe box sukkah** (page 76 in *Integrating Arts and Crafts in the Jewish School*).

3. **Teach your students how to wave the lulav properly and to recite the appropriate blessings.**

4. **Make an illustrated booklet or chart of the special Sukkot blessings.**

5. **Make a mural depicting the various things we do to celebrate Sukkot.**

6. **Plan a tzedakah project having to do with collecting food for the poor.**

7. **Songs for Sukkot:**

"B'Sukkah Shelanu" from *The New Children's Songbook*, edited by Velvel Pasternak (Tara Publications, 1981), p. 20.

"Harvest Song" and "What's Our Sukkah For?" from *The New Jewish Songbook* by H. Coopersmith (Behrman House, 1965), pp. 12, 14.

FAMILY EDUCATION IDEAS ARE LOCATED AT THE END OF THIS GUIDE

SIMHAT TORAH

Important Concepts

1. On Simhat Torah we demonstrate our love for Torah. We sing and dance as we carry the Torah around the synagogue. We wave flags and eat sweets.

2. On Simhat Torah we complete the reading of the last portion of Deuteronomy (the final portion of the Torah) and immediately begin the reading again with the first portion of Genesis (the first portion of the Torah).

3. The Torah contains commandments, or *mitzvot*, that teach us how to live. It also contains stories of the lives of our ancestors.

4. Each Torah is made by hand with the same materials that have been used for centuries.

5. The Torah contains five books: Genesis, Exodus, Leviticus, Numbers, and Deuteronomy.

6. Each week we read a new portion of the Torah until we finish reading the entire scroll. This takes one full year.

Vocabulary

Aron Hakodesh The Hebrew word *aron* means "closet" or large cabinet. *Kodesh* means "holy." The *Aron Hakodesh* is a special cabinet used to store the Torah.

Hakkafot On Simhat Torah, the Torah is taken from the ark and carried around the synagogue seven times. These parades are referred to as *hakkafot*.

Mitzvot A *mitzvah* is a commandment. The Torah contains 613 mitzvot that we are commanded to observe; some are things we should do, and some are things we shouldn't do; some involve ethical behavior, while others deal with the issues of ordinary daily life.

Sofer The name for the person who writes the Torah, the *klaf* (parchment) inside the mezuzzah, or the klaf inside tefillin. A sofer trains as an apprentice to an experienced sofer for many years in order to learn his craft. It is a labor of love. For more information on the sofer see the book *Sofer* by Dr. Eric Ray, listed in the Suggested Activities.

Background Information

A Personal Experience

I enjoy "living history" museums, those repositories of Americana where the old blacksmith shop and tinsmith shop are preserved and maintained as they might have been in the eighteenth and nineteenth centuries. Actors and actresses dressed in colonial or pioneer garb demonstrate the forgotten arts of glassblowing, broom-making, and fireplace cookery, using only the authentic tools of those days.

These attractions are fun, for they transport you to another time and place, to a day when modern gadgetry didn't exist, when women's fashions were long and frilly, and when Noah Webster was writing the first dictionary. There is something romantic about that world—the steam engines, the horse carts, the old plows and farm tools—yet today these things are merely curiosities, relics of the past. They are nothing more than remnants of our history, curiosities that help us remember whence we've come.

Our Torah, too, is a reminder of our past. A series of books compiled long before Noah Webster's first dictionary, our Torah is still made by hand just as it was in the days of Ezra the Scribe (500 B.C.E.). The Torah is penned with a quill, the scribe making sure each word, each column, exactly matches those in every other Torah.

The Torah might seem like a relic or curiosity to some who study us from the outside, but to a Jew, the Torah is the living symbol of our connection to God. We no longer build steam engines or cotton gins, but we keep writing new Sifre-Torah. And we use them. We read them. We study them. We turn to the holy words over and over again, and we try to live them. Unlike the memorabilia of our past, Torah is considered not a historic look at what once was, but rather a vision of what we might become.

Beginning the Torah Again

Every year we read the Torah aloud, from beginning to end. It is divided into 56 portions, and each week we take it out in synagogue and read one section (parashah), sometimes two, until the last week, when we read of the death of Moses. After reading the final portion, we roll the scroll directly to the beginning again and read about the birth of the world. Perhaps we don't want to accept the finality of Moses' death, and so we go directly to creation, reassuring ourselves that life's cycle continues. Thus we affirm the continuation of Torah.

My children used to watch a videotape of the story *Alice in Wonderland*. Alice would fall down the rabbit hole almost every day in our house. She would visit the Mock

Turtle, the Cheshire Cat, the Queen of Hearts, and when she would awake at the end to find that it was all a dream, the children would hit the rewind button, and Alice would be back down the rabbit hole before she had time to yawn or stretch. This is what we do on Simhat Torah. We hit rewind as soon as we are done, never giving ourselves time to emerge from the world of Torah. Moses dies, but he is immediately reborn as the world is recreated. It is for this event that we celebrate. It is for this that we dance and sing.

A Historical Perspective

In the days of the Talmud, Sukkot lasted seven days and was followed by the two-day holiday of Shemini Atzeret. On the second day of Shemini Atzeret it was customary to read the last two chapters of Deuteronomy, which deal with the death of Moses. This was done not because the Torah was being completed on that day, because in Talmudic times the Torah was read on a triennial cycle, meaning it took three years to finish the full Torah. It just happened that the death of Moses was chosen as the special reading for that day.

Later, the Geonim, the rabbinic scholars of Babylon (sixth to eleventh centuries), created the custom of the annual cycle of readings, divided the Torah into 56 *parshiot* or portions, and created the special celebration of Simhat Torah. The Geonim also began the custom of reading sections from Joshua (which continues the story of our people after Moses' death) for the haftarah portion.

Some theorize that after the destruction of the Temple in 70 C.E., when there was no more water pouring ceremony (see Sukkot), no more pageantry, no more great festival of gathering, people felt that they were left with a void. The water pouring festival was said to be the highlight of the year, and with that gone, something needed to take its place. Perhaps Simhat Torah, the holiday of "Joy in the Torah," came about to fill just such a void.

Celebrating in the Synagogue

During the Simhat Torah service, all the Sifre-Torah are removed from the ark. We dance and sing and carry the Torah around the bimah, around the synagogue, and even outside.

It is customary to make seven *hakkafot*, or circlings, with the Torah. With the seven days of Sukkot, the seven guests that visit the Sukkah, and the seven days of creation (including Shabbat, the day of rest), the rabbis seemed enamored with this number.

The Torah is read on erev (evening of) Simhat Torah as well as in the morning. This is the only day of the year when reading the Torah in the evening is permissible in Orthodox and Conservative congregations.

Deuteronomy 33:1-27 is read over and over in order to enable everyone to have an aliyah. Even children can be called for an aliyah. There is a tradition of calling *kol ha-n'arim* (all the youngsters) under the age of Bar/Bat Mitzvah. They stand on the bimah with a large tallit stretched over their heads. An adult helps them with the Torah blessing, after which the entire congregation recites Jacob's blessing over Menasheh and Ephraim (Genesis 48:16-20). When girls are blessed, the names Sarah, Rebecca, Rachel, and Leah are often added.

The great honor of reading the very last section of Deuteronomy and the very first section of Genesis is given to two worthy individuals. They are called the *Hatan Torah* (literally, bridegroom of the Torah) and the *Hatan Bereshit* (the bridegroom of Genesis). As the Hatan Torah finishes the last section of Deuteronomy, the entire congregation recites, "*Hazak, hazak v'nithazek!*" "Be strong, be strong. Let us strengthen each other!" This phrase is chanted whenever a book of the Torah is completed during the year.

There are a few traditional songs that are sung on Simhat Torah, though any song that has to do with the Torah is usable. "*Sisu v'simhu b'Simhat Torah,*" "Be glad and rejoice on Simhat Torah" is a very popular one. After the service, jelly apples, ice cream, or other sweet treats are served to the congregation, especially to the children.

It has become the custom in many synagogues to use the occasion of Simhat Torah as the day when consecration is celebrated. This is a special ceremony to welcome the youngest school-age members of the congregation into their new world of religious school. These youngsters are usually called to the bimah, are given a small part such as saying the Shema, and are then blessed by the rabbi or the entire congregation. They are often given a small toy Torah as a symbol of their Jewish education. At my congregation we give each child a small paper plate with a dab of honey on it. We then ask the children to write in the honey the first Hebrew letter they learned. While the children are making the letter, we recite, "May the study of Torah always be as sweet to you as the honey on your fingers today." The children end up licking their fingers and having a good time.

There are many ways to facilitate the celebration of Simhat Torah. Organizing the hakkafot can be fun as well as intellectually stimulating. See the section on Family Education for some ideas on how this can be done.

Finally, it is interesting to note that during the 1960s Simhat Torah became a day of solidarity for the Jews who lived in Leningrad, Riga, Moscow, and other cities in

Russia. These Jews did not attend synagogue during the year and were unable to express any religious feelings publicly. Yet on Simhat Torah, as a symbol that they had not forgotten who they were, they would gather outside the synagogues to sing Jewish songs and dance horas. At first the authorities tried to disperse the crowds, but as the Jews swelled into the tens of thousands, the authorities had to look the other way. The people's need to be together and to celebrate had prevailed.

Introducing the Lesson

Ask your students if they have any favorite books or videotapes that they read or listen to over and over again. Let them respond by describing their favorites.

Ask them why they like to hear the stories over and over. Why isn't one time enough? List their reasons. They might be something like: "I feel good when I read my favorite book . . . ." "I like the part where . . . ." Most will say simply "Because I like it" or "I hate when it's over."

Explain that we have similar feelings about the Torah. We read it, and when we are through we roll it back to the beginning and start to read it all over again. Ask the class why they think we do this. They should answer, "Because we like it" or "Because we want to hear a special part again." Explain that Simhat Torah is a lot like pressing the rewind button on the VCR. When we are done we go straight back to the beginning because we love the Torah and we don't ever want to finish it. We want it to continue forever.

Tell the class that Simhat Torah is the day when we celebrate our love for Torah by finishing the reading and then rewinding so that we can immediately begin again.

Teaching the Text

The Torah Scroll The Torah is a book that unrolls, just as all books did in ancient days. The parchment is made of animal skin, sewn together with the sinew of the leg of a kosher animal. The ink is of carbon, gallnut powder, gum arabic, and copper sulfate. It is applied with a quill pen. Metal is not used to make a Torah, for metal is used to make weapons of war. The parchment for the Torah comes from animals that have already been killed for food or died of natural causes.

On the Torah we place a mantle, a cloth covering, that is quite ornate. In addition there is a breastplate and a *keter* (crown), or *rimonim* (the round silver tops). Over the top we hang a *yad* (pointer, literally "hand"). We use the yad to keep our place while reading. We don't want to smudge the special ink with our fingers.

Five Books of Torah The Hebrew names for the books of the Torah are not direct translations of the English. The Hebrew names come from the first important word in each book. The first Hebrew word of the book Genesis is *Bereshit* (literally "in the beginning"), and so we refer to Genesis in Hebrew as *Bereshit.*

There are 56 Torah portions to read throughout year. Sometimes there is a double portion, and sometimes there is a special holiday portion that is read out of order.

In the Synagogue On Simhat Torah all the scrolls are removed from the ark for the celebration. Tell your students that on Simhat Torah they can have an aliyah just like the adults. They should practice the Torah blessing. Also you can review some of the choreography of the Torah service. When the Torah is taken from the ark, it is paraded around the congregation. Everyone has the opportunity to touch and kiss it as it goes by. See the Background Information for more details on the special customs for the Torah reading on Simhat Torah.

Joy in the Torah Ask the class on what other occasions we dance for joy (weddings, Bar/Bat Mitzvahs, parties).

Suggested Activities

1. **Read and discuss the book** *Sofer*, by Dr. Eric Ray (Los Angeles: Torah Aura, 1986). It describes the story of a present-day scribe and the work he does to make a Torah. It is full of information on how a Torah is made and contains interesting photographs.

2. **Have the children make Simhat Torah flags.** Thin wooden dowels can be purchased at hardware stores or lumber outlets. You can staple paper to them to complete the flag. Use the word "Yisrael" in Hebrew to illustrate the flag; you can even print it with crowns, like the letters that are written in the Torah. The children can then draw on the flags pictures of Israel or an illustration of a Bible story.

3. **Take your class into the sanctuary to examine the Torah scrolls.** Point out how the Torah is made, and tell the names of the different parts. Always ask the children to treat the Torah with the respect that a holy object deserves. This includes touching the text only with the yad.

4. **Unroll a toy Torah in your classroom to see how long it is.**

5. **Teach your class to dance the hora.**

6. **Make a simple Torah using two unsharpened pencils and a roll of long white paper.** Divide the paper into sections and have the children illustrate them with the different Torah scenes that they have learned.

7. **Teach the children the Torah blessing so that they can be called to the bimah on Simhat Torah.**

8. **Prepare jelly apples.**

9. **Sing songs for Simhat Torah.** "Sisu V'simcha" and "Yom Tov Lanu" are from *The New Jewish Songbook* by H. Coopersmith (West Orange, NJ: Behrman House, 1965).

FAMILY EDUCATION IDEAS ARE LOCATED AT THE END OF THIS GUIDE

SHABBAT

(Text pages 56-71)

Important Concepts

1. We celebrate Shabbat every seven days. It is a day of rest for God, for people, even for animals.

2. We learn about Shabbat from the creation story in the Torah. In that story God works for six days to create the world and rests on the seventh.

3. The commandment to keep the Sabbath is one of the Ten Commandments.

4. We prepare for the Sabbath every Friday by cooking, cleaning, and finishing our chores for the week.

5. We mark the beginning of Shabbat at sundown on Friday by lighting Shabbat candles and saying the proper blessing. We also say the Kiddush over wine and Hamotzi over hallah.

6. We pray together in synagogue on Friday night and Saturday morning. On Saturday morning the Torah is read.

7. We end Shabbat on Saturday evening with a special ceremony called Havdalah.

Vocabulary

Birkat Hamazon This series of blessings recited after a meal is several pages long in its unedited form. Both the Conservative and Reform movements offer abbreviated versions for home and synagogue use. The booklet that contains the Birkat Hamazon is known informally as a *bencher*.

Eliyahu Hanavi Eliyahu is the Hebrew name for Elijah, and a *navi* is a prophet. Elijah is the prophet who is said to roam the earth, helping those in need, appearing at every brit and at every Passover seder. He is said to be the one who will herald the coming of the Messiah at the end of days.

Hallah The special bread we eat on Shabbat. It is braided for Shabbat but round for Rosh Hashanah. The *Encyclopedia Judaica* (Vol. 6, p. 1419) has a page showing the variety of shapes hallah can take on different occasions.

Hamotzi This blessing which we recite before eating bread thanks God for bringing forth bread from the earth.

Havdalah The ceremony that separates the Sabbath from the rest of the week. We use this ceremony to separate the sacred from the mundane. Objects that are used during Havdalah include a tall braided candle, wine, and fragrant spices.

Kiddush Kiddush comes from the Hebrew root that means "holy." This blessing recited over wine makes the wine holy.

L'cha Dodi A poem written by Solomon Alkabez in the 1600s. It draws the analogy between Shabbat and a beautiful bride dressed in white.

Oneg Shabbat The Hebrew word *oneg* means "joy." One way we express our joy on Shabbat is to eat festive foods together. The Oneg Shabbat after the Friday night service offers us this opportunity.

Shalom This complex Hebrew word is used as the word for peace. It comes from the Hebrew root *shalem,* which means wholeness. As a result, the word *shalom* conveys a sense of feeling whole and together, rather than just simply peaceful.

Background Information

A Gift to the World

The Sabbath has been called the Jewish gift to the world. The Greeks and Romans had no Sabbath. They worked seven days a week and made fun of the Jews for what they called laziness. Yet, in modern days, almost every country in the world has adopted some version of the six-day work week. The concept of a "day off," of Shabbat, is one of our unique contributions to civilization.

The body needs refreshment, rest, and diversion. But a true Shabbat refreshes more than the body. Observed correctly, a day of rest should revive and nourish the soul as well. We put aside our work, our chores, our routines, as well as our cares and stresses. On Shabbat we put our ambitions on hold: our quests for money or power, and our desires to change and alter our planet. We do this in order to spend time with our thoughts and dreams, to enjoy learning, nature, and the company of family and friends.

Three times the Torah reminds us to keep the Sabbath. Two of these are in connection with creation, and one is in connection with the Exodus from Egypt. The first two remind us that we too are creators, builders, and shapers who must carefully consider the consequences of each new construction. The third mention of keeping the Sabbath reminds us always to be cognizant of the needs of others, especially the oppressed, for we too were once slaves in Egypt. As it is written in Exodus 20:8-11: "Remember Shabbat and keep it holy . . . . Remember that you were a slave in the land of Egypt and the Lord your God freed you from there with a mighty hand and an outstretched arm; therefore the Lord your God has commanded you to observe the Sabbath day." Shabbat helps us to focus on what the world can one day become and on what we are capable of doing to create that perfect world.

Observing Shabbat in Today's World

Building a lifestyle that revolves around Shabbat observance in our modern world can be very challenging. Sometimes I feel as though I am at war with the Girl Scout leader, the soccer coach, the school P.T.A., and the list goes on and on. There is no end to the number of Saturday events to which my family says no during the year. Sometimes we say no easily and sometimes not. Each time my children feel that they are being singled out once again as different—the Jewish kid. It is no wonder that so many Jews have begun to give up their Shabbat observance for activities of the non-Jewish world. These outside influences can easily conspire to drag us away from who we are and what we should be.

How do we keep this from happening? I don't pretend to have the answers. Yet we all make choices—conscious, deliberate choices for ourselves and for our children. We simply need to consider more carefully the consequences of these decisions as we make them—not just how they will affect us today, but, in a broader sense, how they will affect our attitudes, our children's future attitudes, and the general health of our family's lifestyle. I think it is one of our major goals as Jewish educators to try to bring more Shabbat into our lives, and in turn into the lives of the families with whom we work. This is no easy task, but we also need to ask ourselves, can Judaism survive without the Sabbath?

Shabbat in the Bible

Shabbat is mentioned over and over in the Torah. It is explained in the creation story (God worked for six days and rested on the seventh), but is not mentioned by name. Later, the character of this special day is expounded upon in the story of the manna in the wilderness. As the Jews wandered in the desert, God supplied their food by dropping manna from heaven. For five days each person was provided with one portion, but a double portion was collected on the sixth so that no work would need to be done on the Sabbath (Exodus 16:22).

Exodus 23:12 tells us that work is to cease on the Sabbath to give slaves and farm animals a rest. Deuteronomy 5:14-15 expresses this same sentiment and adds that God, who liberated us from Egyptian bondage, commands us to observe the Sabbath and cease from work. Numbers 28:9-10 tells us that an additional sacrificial offering was expected on the Sabbath. From this we have the additional (Musaf) service that we still hold on Shabbat as a reminder of the additional Temple sacrifice.

Shabbat Throughout History

After the destruction of the Temple in 70 C.E. the Sabbath became a very important vehicle of Jewish expression in a Gentile world. This distinctive holiday separated the Jews from those with whom they lived, and so Shabbat was given a role of greater importance. It was seen then, as now, as a barrier to assimilation.

Later in history we read the book of Maccabees and find that during one battle the Maccabees chose to be killed rather than offer resistance on the Sabbath. Rabbinic literature is also full of references to the Sabbath. Exodus Rabbah 25:12 in the Talmud states, "If Israel keeps one Sabbath as it should be kept, the Messiah will come. The Sabbath is equal to all the other precepts of the Torah."

Shabbat Dinner

When a family gathers at the Sabbath table, it is traditional to empty their pockets of coins to symbolize that they will not be engaging in business during the next day. The coins are put in a tzedakah box.

The Sabbath begins with the lighting of at least two candles. There must be at least two because they represent the two acts to "remember" and "observe," as the commandment is stated in the Torah. The candles are lit shortly before sundown, and then the proper blessing is recited. Many people cover their eyes until after the blessing is said in order to shield their eyes from the light of a mitzvah done before the recitation of the blessing. (Generally, blessings are recited before the mitzvah is performed.)

A festive meal is set with two braided hallot as the centerpiece. The two hallot remind us of the double portion of manna that God offered in the wilderness for the Sabbath. Some people who bake their own hallah observe the following custom: They remove a small ball of dough to burn in the oven as a reminder of the sacrifices of Shabbat in the days of the Temple.

When the candles are lit "Shalom Aleichem" is sung, and the Kiddush is recited over the wine. Some people perform the mitzvah of washing their hands with the proper blessing. This can be done at the table with a basin and a special cup or it can be done at the kitchen sink. The Hamotzi is recited, and a bit of salt is sprinkled on the bread. Everyone is quiet until each person has sampled a piece of bread. At this point the children are blessed.

There is a traditional blessing that husbands say for their wives called Eshet Hayil, Woman of Valor. It praises the woman for her industriousness and thanks her for all the patient work she did on everyone's behalf that week. The Reform book, *Gates of the Home,* also now contains an additional, similar passage to be recited on behalf of the man in the family.

After a festive meal, the Birkat Hamazon (The Blessings of the Meal) is said. The Birkat should be said after any meal that begins with Hamotzi, but it is nice to make a special effort to remember to say it on Shabbat. This is usually followed by a song session at the table. Each family has their favorites.

In the Synagogue

Services for Shabbat are held in the synagogue on both Friday night and Saturday morning. Orthodox and some Conservative synagogues hold a "Kabbalat Shabbat" service that begins at sunset on Friday evening. As it concludes, congregants recite Kiddush and then return home for dinner. Reform synagogues and some Conservative congregations hold a later Friday evening service that concludes with an Oneg Shabbat, a festive collation to honor the Sabbath. Tea and cake are served as people socialize.

At the Saturday morning service, the Torah is taken out and read. Seven aliyot are called, and the eight-blessing Amidah is recited, shortened from the nineteen blessings on weekdays. Some synagogues read the entire portion for the week, those that read on the triennial cycle read one third of the portion, and some read only enough for one aliyah. Hallah, fish, and cake are usually served after this service. It is also at this morning service that most B'nai Mitzvah ceremonies take place.

After services, it is customary to have a festive lunch. Many prefer to prepare the food the day before so as not to have to work on the Sabbath. Dishes such as cholent and tsimmes were born from this custom. They are pots of various stews that are cooked for hours in a warm oven that was left on the night before.

After lunch one can take a nap, visit with friends, read, study Torah, or otherwise relax. Permissible activities are very specific for Orthodox Jews and subject to interpretation for Conservative and Reform Jews. One is supposed to keep one's activities within the spirit of Shabbat, however, and choose things that offer tranquility of mind and spirit.

Many synagogues offer an afternoon service called *minchah,* and a *seudah shlishit* or "third meal." It is a mitzvah to eat three meals over the course of the Sabbath as a festive way of celebrating the day.

Havdalah

When three stars appear in the sky, it is time for Havdalah, the ceremony that separates the Sabbath from the rest of the week. We light a tall braided candle, recite Kiddush over wine, smell sweet spices, and let the light of the candle reflect on our hands. We recite a blessing before each of these acts, hoping that the sweet smell of Shabbat, symbolized by the spices, will follow us into the new week. When we sing "Eliyahu Hanavi," we recall the promise that one day the Messiah will come, heralded by Elijah the Prophet. At the conclusion of the Havdalah ceremony we dip the candle into the remaining wine and, as it is extinguished, we wish our friends and family *Shavuah Tov,* "a good week."

Introducing the Lesson

You might wish to introduce this lesson with a brief story. Following are three suggested ones. You can simply tell the story, or you can use puppets or a felt board to aid your presentation. While there are many stories that teach the concept of Shabbat rest, the following is one of my favorites:

Once upon a time there was a farmer. He had two oxen that lived in his barn. Every day the oxen would work with the farmer in the fields, pulling his plow across the earth to grow grain for the winter. They would work from morning until night. The oxen were hitched to the front of the plow, and the farmer steered from behind. The sun was hot, the plow was heavy, and each evening they would return to the barn tired and thirsty after a hard day of work.

This would occur for six days, but on the evening of the sixth day the farmer would bring the oxen extra food and water, give them extra warm, cozy blankets for their comfort, and wish them a "good Shabbas." Neither the farmer nor the oxen worked on the seventh day, for that was the Sabbath, a day of rest for all God's creatures. The farmer and the oxen loved the Sabbath, for it gave them a chance to rest from their difficult work, and when the Sabbath was over, they felt refreshed and ready to work again.

And so it went. The farmer and the oxen got along well, for each felt that his needs were being met. They worked and rested, and they prospered together.

Unfortunately, there came a year when the crops failed, when there was not enough water to grow the grain, and the farmer did not have enough money to feed the two oxen their hay. He needed a way to raise some money so he could get through the coming winter.

One of the neighboring farmers had offered to buy one of the oxen for use on his farm. Our poor friend felt he had no choice but to sell one of his oxen for money to use during the winter. So one fall morning the farmer and the ox bid each other a sad good-bye as the new owner came to bring the ox to his new home.

The remaining ox and the farmer missed their friend, but what could they do? They needed to buy food for the winter.

Meanwhile, the ox at his new home was not happy. This new farmer did not keep the Sabbath. He worked out in the field seven days a week and expected his animals to do the same. The ox was exhausted and became ill. After several weeks the ox had had enough. On the next Sabbath he refused to leave his stall in the barn. He refused to work, and no matter what the man tried to do to get the animal out of the stall, he just wouldn't go. This made the man terribly angry.

"I paid good money for you so that you would work for me! Yet you are lazy and sick, a good-for-nothing! That farmer sold me a rotten ox, and I am going to give you back." The man put a rope around the ox's neck and angrily led him back to his old home.

"Look at this sick old cow you sold me. He's good for nothing! I demand my money back!"

The farmer looked at his friend the ox. He was thin and weak, and obviously very sad.

"Look what you have done to my ox!" said the farmer. "You have ruined him. By not giving him a chance to rest, you have robbed him of his health and happiness. You are returning damaged goods. For this I can give you back only half your money."

The men agreed. The farmer returned half the money in exchange for the return of his old friend. The farmer took the ox back to his old barn and nursed him back to health. He was glad to have his friend back and was able to use the remaining money to get by during the winter.

The ox began to feel well again and went back to his old routine of working for six days and resting on the seventh, for as it says in the Torah, "Observe Shabbat and keep it holy. . . ."

Another story to begin the lesson with is the creation story. Both Exodus 31:16-17 and Exodus 20:8-11 use the creation story as the explanation of our Sabbath observance. We, acting as God did, work for six days and rest on the seventh. The story itself is found in the very beginning of the Torah, Genesis 1:1-2:3. It is retold in *My Jewish Year* at the beginning of the Shabbat chapter, pages 58-59. The following are suggested activities you might want to do with your class after reading the creation story.

1. Choose seven children to line up in front of the class. Each one acts out a different day of creation as you narrate the story from the text.

2. Write each day's creation on a separate index card. Shuffle the cards and randomly hand them out to seven children. See if they can line themselves up in the correct order. Have the class check the result.

For craft ideas having to do with the story, see the list of suggested activities at the end of this chapter.

Another good story to begin the lesson on Shabbat is "Sabbath Spice," which can be found on pages 61-62 of *My Jewish Year*. After reading this story with the class, you might wish to lead a brief discussion using the following questions:

1. Why did the rabbi invite the Roman Emperor to eat with him on the Sabbath? (They were friends. The rabbi loved to cook and the emperor loved to eat. It is a mitzvah to prepare for the Sabbath. It is a mitzvah to invite guests for the Sabbath.)

2. Why did the rabbi cook such excellent food? (The rabbi was a good cook. We try to eat our best meal of the week on the Sabbath. The Sabbath made the food taste especially good.)

3. Why was the emperor's cook unable to make the food taste special? (The food was lacking the special Shabbat spice.)

4. What is the Sabbath spice? (The Sabbath spice is the good feeling that we have on this special day. It makes our food taste better. We can eat apples and honey any day, but they taste especially sweet on Rosh Hashanah. We can eat creamy cake any day, but the cake is extra good when it is your birthday. The specialness of the day adds to the specialness of the food.)

You can have the children act out this small story in class. If a holiday is coming up, you might wish to prepare a special food for that holiday, explaining that it will taste extra good when eaten on the special day.

Teaching the Text

When you finish a beautiful painting . . . Explain that even though Shabbat comes more often than the other holidays, it is considered the most important.

Creation See the section Introducing the Lesson.

Looking Back Explain that the shofar was used to announce all the holidays as well as the time of the new moon. You might want to have a shofar to show the class. It is blown in the same manner as a trumpet. Ask someone who knows how to blow shofar to come in and demonstrate its use.

Ask the class how we know when Shabbat begins if we no longer blow the shofar. (We check the candle lighting times on a Jewish calendar or figure out eighteen minutes before sunset on Friday evening.) Explain why the actual candle lighting time is different in different cities across the United States.

The text describes how people used to prepare for Shabbat. Ask the class how we prepare today. (We clean, shop, prepare a nice meal, bake hallah, dress in nice clothing.)

Shabbat Evening at Home Ask the class what else they can do to welcome Shabbat. (Bake hallah, dress in clean clothes, bathe ourselves, clean the house, buy the things we need so we don't have to shop on Saturday, etc.)

Sabbath Spice See the section Introducing the Lesson.

Candles We cover our eyes after we light the candles so that we can't see the light until after we say the blessing. Usually a blessing is said before we do the mitzvah. We light two or more candles, one to show we observe Shabbat, and one to show we remember Shabbat.

Kiddush When we say the Kiddush, we are making our wine into something special. Wine is a substance that in excess is easily abused yet in moderation is something we can enjoy and use as a holy object. Saying Kiddush shows how we can make the ordinary, even the potentially harmful, into something special or holy.

Hallah Why do we say blessings after the meal? (We wish to thank God for the food we have eaten.) We should say the Birkat Hamazon after any meal where Hamotzi is said.

In the Synagogue Ask the children to describe their experiences at children's services on the Sabbath. Use their recollections to add information to the discussion in the text.

Practice using the greeting "Shabbat Shalom" among the group. Learn the deaf hand signs for these words. (Shabbat: the left hand is horizontal, the right hand is in a ball representing the sun. The sun moves down toward the horizon to show the setting of the sun. Shalom: the right hand begins at twelve o'clock and draws a circle in the air that ends at six o'clock.)

Shabbat Afternoon Ask your students, "How does your family celebrate Shabbat?" or "How would you like your family to celebrate Shabbat?"

Havdalah We take special care in Judaism to separate the sacred from the ordinary. This is the specific function of Havdalah, to separate Shabbat from the ordinary days of the week. It is nice at this point to show a Havdalah set and to demonstrate Havdalah for the group. It is a sensory experience that children enjoy and easily remember. We recite the blessing for wine, spices, and the light of the candle.

At the end of Havdalah we remember Elijah the Prophet by singing "Eliyahu Hanavi." Tradition tells us that one day, every day will be as Shabbat, and that when that time comes Elijah will be the herald of this news on earth.

Suggested Activities

1. **Learning the blessings.** There are many blessings mentioned in this chapter. The teacher can make a poster or banner for selected ones, and the class can learn to sing them by heart. Note the suggestions for teaching the blessings in the introduction of this book.

2. **Create a mobile.** For the creation story you can make a Creation Mobile, hanging the objects that your students have made for each day of creation. You could also make a Creation Book with one page devoted to each day of creation, or make a Creation Mural depicting the events of creation on a large piece of paper.

3. **Teach your students how to find Shabbat on a Jewish calendar.** Show your students a Jewish calendar. Locate the days that are Shabbat. See if the calendar lists candle lighting times for different cities.

4. **Make a chart for the classroom that lists the ways we prepare for Shabbat and the things we do to keep Shabbat.**

5. **Make hallah covers with puffy paint or other fabric paints on cloth of your choice.**

6. **Make candlesticks or Kiddush cups.** See pages 53 and 58 in *Integrating Arts and Crafts in the Jewish School.*

FAMILY EDUCATION IDEAS ARE LOCATED AT THE END OF THIS GUIDE

HANUKKAH

(Text pages 72-87)

Important Concepts

1. The holiday of Hanukkah commemorates the rededication of the Holy Temple in Jerusalem by the Maccabees on the 25th day of Kislev in 165 B.C.E. We celebrate the heroism of the Maccabees in the face of religious persecution as well as their zealous opposition to the forces of assimilation.

2. Hanukkah lasts for eight days. On each of the eight nights we light a hanukkiah, or menorah, to remind us of the rededication of the Eternal Light in the ancient Temple.

3. As we light the hanukkiah, we say the proper blessings.

4. We play a special game with a dreidel on Hanukkah.

5. Traditional foods for Hanukkah are foods that have been fried in oil, such as potato latkes.

6. It is customary to exchange small gifts on each of the eight nights of Hanukkah. A gift of money at this time of year is known as "Hanukkah gelt."

Vocabulary

Antiochus Ruler of the Syrian empire at the time of the Maccabean revolt. Antiochus deified himself, calling himself "Epiphanes" or "God made manifest." He took the gold and treasures from the Holy Temple, set Greek idols on the altar, and issued a proclamation declaring that Jews could not keep the Sabbath or study Torah.

Dreidel A four-sided top used in a child's game. Each side of the top contains one Hebrew letter: *nun, gimmel, hay, shin*. They stand for the phrase, "Nes gadol hayah sham," or "A great miracle happened there."

Eternal Light The oil lamp in the Temple that burned day and night. Today, as a reminder of the oil lamp in the Holy Temple, an eternal light (usually electric) hangs in each synagogue above the Aron Hakodesh (Holy Ark).

Gelt The Yiddish word for gold which later broadened its meaning to mean money.

Hanukkiah The Hebrew word for a menorah that holds nine candles.

Judah Heroic son of Mattathias, who led the revolt against the Syrian-Greeks.

Latkes Potato pancakes. They are a traditional Hanukkah food because they are fried in oil.

Maccabees The group of religious zealots who defeated the Syrian-Greeks and rededicated the Holy Temple after its defilement. They were later known as the Hasmoneans and held power for many years after.

Mattathias Father of Judah Maccabee. Mattathias defied Greek authority and began the revolt against Antiochus. He is a prime example of someone who stood up for religious freedom in the face of danger.

Nes Gadol Hayah Sham A phrase meaning "A great miracle happened there." The first letter of each word appears on the dreidel. Dreidels in Israel have one letter that is different. Instead of a *shin* they have a *pay* so that the dreidel reads, "A great miracle happened *here*."

Shamash Shamash comes from the Hebrew root "to use" and literally means the servant or the worker. The shamash is used to light the other candles in the hanukkiah.

Background Information

Hanukkah and Christmas

Each year as Thanksgiving concludes, the calls and requests begin to come in. Christmas fever mounts in schools, churches, businesses, and as our well-meaning neighbors go about their frantic preparations for what is their pivotal theological holiday, they can't help but notice that we are not joining in. Then, with well-motivated multicultural aims, they ask me, "Could you make some time to come in and tell us about your holiday? Hanukkah, isn't it?"

I smile politely as they tell me how someone once gave them a dreidel and they still have it, and how very "neat" it is that we light that special thing, but they forgot the name of the Hanukkah menorah. To the great elation of whomever I am speaking with, I agree to visit the classroom or church, all the while sadly considering that our rich theological past has been reduced, in their minds, to a dreidel.

I wish I had a piece of Hanukkah gelt (the chocolate kind) for every time I have been asked, "Aren't you just exhausted from all your holiday preparations? There's a lot to do to get ready for Hanukkah, isn't there?"

I politely respond, "Not really. Hanukkah is not a major celebration." What the person doesn't realize is that I did feel exhausted in the fall, when our string of major holidays demanded all my time and attention: taking the time in the fall to cook banquet meals, then fast, then build a Sukkah and decorate it, then dance with the Torah, while all the world was going about their business without canceling one single event in order to give us a little more opportunity to celebrate.

Christians rarely realize that Hanukkah is not a major celebration. (And many Jews fall into this category as well.) I do receive polite "Season's Greetings" cards that omit any reference to Jesus, but what would be even more appropriate from someone who is trying to recognize our differences would be a New Year's card in September. Music teachers who wish to sing Christmas carols in public schools ask me for Hanukkah music, unaware that the rich body of Jewish music that exists for Shabbat or Passover might be much more interesting.

Despite all this, my husband and I make the obligatory visits to the schools and churches each year. But rather than focusing on Hanukkah, I take the opportunity to talk about what Jews believe, what we feel, and our yearly cycle of holidays, stressing Rosh Hashanah, Yom Kippur, Shabbat, and Passover. I bring in Jewish objects, teach a little Hebrew, and talk about what Israel means to us.

I love Hanukkah. I love the message, the lights, the gifts, the happy children. Hanukkah should be a meaningful, well-celebrated time for all Jews. But it should not be the only thing a Jewish family does all year, and it should never be considered an event comparable to Christmas. To do this belittles an important Christian holiday as well as all the other marvelous Jewish experiences our year provides.

How Did the Hanukkah Celebration Begin?

The month of Tishre, with all its various holidays, is now behind us. Heshvan passes with no special events. The weather gets cold and the days dark. As we approach the winter solstice, Hanukkah looms on the horizon, the "Festival of Lights."

Some Jewish sources choose to minimize the fact that Hanukkah and the solstice come at the same time of year. They wish to distance Jewish celebration from anything that might be of pagan origin. And it is true that we celebrate Hanukkah on the 25th of Kislev, the exact date of the rededication of the Temple by the Maccabees as recorded in the book of Maccabees. Josephus, a historian of the Bar Kochba era who lived about 100 years after the rededication of the Temple, has written that he does not know why the festival is called "Lights." Apparently, at the time of Josephus there were no lights connected with the celebration of the holiday.

Some modern historians espouse the very interesting theory that Hanukkah began as a late celebration of Sukkot. During the three years of the Maccabean revolt, Jews did not have access to the Holy Temple. They celebrated Sukkot in the mountains, building booths and waving the lulav, but they were unable to fulfill their obligation to bring sacrifices to the Temple. When the Temple was rededicated a few months after Sukkot, the Maccabees wished to recelebrate Sukkot in the proper fashion. That is why, these historians explain, Hanukkah lasts for eight days, just like Sukkot with Shemini Atzeret. That is why it was originally suggested (by Shammai) that we start with eight candles and light one less each day, rather than the other way around, for one less each day was the way sacrifices were brought to the Temple on Sukkot. (Hillel, the opposing opinion, suggested that we light one more candle each night so as to increase our joy as the days progress. We now follow the opinion of Rabbi Hillel.) It is interesting to note that there is no mention of lights in the Books of Maccabees, the principal historical reference we have concerning the events of this era.

The Hanukkah Story

The period of time in Jewish history that Hanukkah commemorates is one of the most fascinating in our entire past. The Maccabees, represented by Mattathias, the elderly patriarch, and his five sons, Judah, Eliezer, Shimon, Yochanan, and Yonatan, were religious zealots of their day, refusing to bow to the pressure to assimilate into Greek culture. Just as is the case today, Jews were living within a dominant, alien culture, absorbing some of its elements and rejecting others, especially when these were in opposition to Jewish law. Some of the Greek culture was beneficial to the Jews, such as the advances in mathematics, music, the arts, and politics. Yet much of Greek culture required the abandonment of Jewish law. Greek food involved the eating of nonkosher animals, and general participation in Greek life required the abandonment of the Sabbath. Ultimately, King Antiochus, the Syrian-Greek ruler, decided that his kingdom would function better with an assimilated population. He outlawed the study of Jewish texts, circumcision, kosher food, and Shabbat observance. Many Jews who were enamored by the beauty of Greek culture obeyed the decree, but others, who were more committed to Torah, were furious.

Rallying under the leadership of the Maccabees, the Jews fought a three-year war against the Syrian-Greeks in order to regain their freedom to worship as Jews. Their main goal was to liberate the Holy Temple in Jerusalem, which had been defiled by the Greeks. Greek statues had been brought into the Temple, and pagan sacrifices took place there. On the 25th of Kislev in 166 B.C.E. the army of the Maccabees were able to enter the gates of the Holy Temple once more. They found the place in a shambles, the gates burnt, the courtyard overgrown. They tore their garments, as is the mourning practice, put ashes on their heads, and then proceeded to rebuild the Temple.

The word Hanukkah means "dedication," and on the 25th of Kislev the Temple was rededicated with the renewal of the daily sacrificial service, the singing of songs, the playing of musical instruments, and the chanting of Hallel. According to the book of Maccabees, a new altar had been built, and the seven-branched menorah was restored.

The Maccabees, later known as the Hasmoneans, became the rulers of the Land of Israel. They held power from the time of the rededication of the Temple in 166 B.C.E. until the destruction of the Temple by the Romans in 70 C.E. By that time their regime had been corrupted by personal vendettas and struggles for power, a sad ending for such a valiant struggle.

Later on, as the Mishnah was being compiled (circa 185-200 C.E.), the rabbis chose not to include a word about Hanukkah. Furthermore, the books of the Maccabees were not canonized in the Bible. Why? Perhaps the rabbis did not want to glorify a military victory. Perhaps they did not want to glorify those who were from a different ruling dynasty than themselves. After all, the Hasmoneans had crowned themselves kings and were not from the line of David.

Noticing the great popularity of the festival, however, the rabbis could not eliminate it. Instead they tried to offer a new interpretation. Shabbat 21a of the Gemara tells us the story of the jar of oil that was to burn for one day but miraculously burned for eight, thereby imbuing the event with a sense of God's intervention. Now it was God as well as Judah Maccabee who had saved the Jews.

The Hanukkiah

The Eternal Light that burned both in the Tent of Meeting of the wandering Israelites and in the Temple in Jerusalem was a seven-branched menorah in the shape of a tree. It burned with olive oil, not candles. The hanukkiah has nine branches, eight for the requirements of the festival, and one—the shamash—to be used to light the others. There are no rules regarding the shape or material used to make a hanukkiah. They are as diverse as the Jews who design them. Many are beautiful works of art.

Each night we light the shamash along with one candle on the first night, two the second, and so on. In addition to lighting the candles we say two blessings, plus the Sheheheyanu on the first night. We add new candles from the left to the right but light them from the right to the left. We also sing or recite the paragraph "Hanerot halalu," which describes how we recall the miracles that our ancestors experienced in days of old.

It also tells us that we are to observe the light but not use it for any purpose of work. We are to place the hanukkiah in the window for all to see so that everyone is reminded of the miracle. Exceptions to this practice were permitted during times when there might have been danger associated with letting others know that a household was observing the Jewish festival.

Celebrating at Home

"Ma'oz Tzur" is commonly sung after the hanukkiah is lit. The Hebrew text describes a number of events in Jewish history that required God's intervention to save our people. The melody comes from Western Europe.

It is customary to play games as the candles burn. Card games are common, as is the dreidel game. (See pages 83-84 of *My Jewish Year* for the rules of this game.)

Foods that are fried in oil are commonly served on Hanukkah. Potato latkes are popular among Eastern European Jews, and doughnuts, known as *sufganiot*, are common among the Jews of the Middle East.

In recent years it has become the custom to give gifts on each of the eight nights of Hanukkah. The gifts have become more lavish with the years, though it has been a long-standing custom to give children "Hanukkah gelt" (money) as a special treat on the holiday. My father, who came from Eastern Europe, used to tell how he looked forward to receiving an orange for Hanukkah. This special fruit was not commonly available and was therefore considered a very special treat. It was the only orange he ate all year.

Each family needs to develop its own standard of gift giving. For some suggestions, see the Family Education section of this Guide.

In the Synagogue

In synagogue the Torah is read on each of the eight days of Hanukkah. The portions come from Numbers, 7 and 8. There is a special haftarah for the Shabbat that falls during Hanukkah: Zechariah 2:14-4:7. It describes a mystical vision of the dedication of the Temple and includes the famous quote, "Not by might and not by power, but by My spirit, says the Lord of hosts." This phrase once again calls to mind that the miraculous victory of Hanukkah was due to the will of God.

In Israel, a popular tradition is a torchlight marathon running from the town of Modin, where the Maccabees lived, to the city of Jerusalem. There the giant menorah is lit to remind us of the miracle that occurred long ago.

Introducing the Lesson

Begin by explaining that it is usually a good idea to follow rules and accept regulations that are imposed upon us by parents, school officials, government, and so on. But there are exceptions when we know that a rule or regulation is wrong. At those times we need to speak out against it, rather than just to continue doing the wrong thing.

Come to class prepared to relate an experience you had when you were forced to speak out against something you felt was wrong. Try to make it something on the students' level so that they will be able to appreciate it fully.

An example might be:

"One day, when I was in second grade, my teacher had to leave the room for a few minutes. The class became very noisy, but I sat and read my book. When the teacher returned, she punished the entire class by not allowing us to go out for recess. I was mad because I hadn't done anything wrong, but I was afraid to tell the teacher.

"When I went home that evening, I told my parents what had happened. They suggested I write a note to my teacher explaining my point of view. I did, and the teacher later apologized to me for not realizing that I had behaved properly."

Let the children tell a few stories, and then relate them to the experiences of Judah Maccabee, who had to defy authority in order to uphold the Torah.

Teaching the Story

Long, long ago . . . Explain that in the days of the Maccabees Jews prayed at the Holy Temple in Jerusalem. Even if they lived far away they went to the Temple three times a year. Ask the students if they can guess which three holidays were the ones that required Jews to go to the Holy Temple (Sukkot, Passover, Shavuot).

Many Jews also followed Greek ways . . . What were some Greek things that Jews began to do? (Speak and read Greek, study Greek art and music, play Greek games, learn Greek math.) Do we do some Christian things because we live near many Christians? In what ways is this good? In what ways is this not a good thing? (Try to steer the discussion toward expressing that we can learn from others and absorb new things as long as we don't compromise ourselves and our beliefs.) You can also express that it is important for others to learn from us.

Antiochus commanded: The Jews may no longer study . . . Have the class look at the list of prohibitions on page 75 of *My Jewish Year* and discuss why each is so important to the Jewish people.

The wicked king and his soldiers . . . Define the word "idol" and talk about what it means to pray to an idol. Discuss the second commandment and point out how idol worship is prohibited in Judaism because we know that God cannot be a statue. You might want to tell the story of Abraham in the idol factory or bring in archaeological pictures of idols.

In a small town . . . Did Mattathias want to be like the Greeks? (No.) What was important to Mattathias? (The Torah.) Do we ever have to stand up for what we believe in? Give examples. (When we are asked to go to a party or a ball game on the Sabbath or on Yom Kippur. When someone makes fun of us because we are Jewish. When our teacher is singing a Christmas song about Jesus and we don't want to sing those words.)

But Judah and the Maccabees . . . There are many stories about Judah in battle. One says that Judah captured the beautiful sword of one of the Syrian generals and used that sword for the rest of his life.

The Legend of the Oil Describe the cleaning of the Temple. Explain the symbolism of the Eternal Light. Look at the one in your sanctuary. Also examine the menorah in your sanctuary. It probably has seven branches. Ask the children why is has seven and not nine branches as the Hanukkah menorah does. (The seven-branched menorah is like the one that stood in the Holy Temple before there even was a Hanukkah.)

Explain how the story about the little jar of oil shows us that the victory of the Maccabees involved the efforts of God and humans working together.)

There is another midrash that tells us that when Judah came to the Temple, he stuck spears into the ground and put lights on them to form the first menorah.

Teaching the Text

The Festival of Lights Have the children bring in or describe the hanukkiah they have at home. Point out the similarities and differences among them. The only requirement for a hanukkiah is that it has to hold nine candles, one of which is set apart. The candles must be able to burn for at least a half hour. Older hanukkiot burned with olive oil instead of candles.

Teach the direction in which we add the candles to the hanukkiah, and the direction in which we light them. Practice the blessings. See the section at the beginning of this Guide, Teaching the Blessings, for ideas.

Dreidel The dreidel game can be played with pennies, nuts, candies, or other items. Each child has a pot of whatever the item is. Everyone at the table places one in the center. One by one the players spin, adding or removing from the pot as their dreidel tells them. At the end of the game, the player with the greatest number of items is the winner.

Latkes Perhaps you would like to cook potato latkes with your class. There are many recipes for this tasty dish.

Hanukkah Gelt Explain the meaning of the word *gelt*. Ask the children what sort of gifts they like to give. Ask if they can come up with ways for your class to give something to the poor.

Suggested Activities

1. **Make a dreidel.** A simple way to do this is to cut cardboard squares about four inches in width. Draw two diagonal lines across each square, forming an X. Draw one Hebrew letter in each triangular space on the square (*nun, gimmel, hay, shin*). Have the children decorate each triangle of the dreidel. Poke a small, sharpened pencil through the center of the X. The dreidels spin very nicely.

2. **Make a home decoration.** Glue popsicle sticks into the shape of Jewish stars. (Make two triangles, then glue them together.) Decorate with glitter and glue. Put a string through the top and hang one on each doorknob of the house.

3. **Make a Hanukkah paperweight.** Each child will need a baby food jar with a lid, and a small plastic dreidel. Glue the dreidel onto the inside of the jar lid. Fill the jar with water and add soap flakes for a snowy effect. Screw the lid on tight, but only after the glue is dry. Turn the jar upside down, and it will snow on the dreidel.

4. **Making menorahs.** There are as many ways to make menorahs as there are Jews on this earth. I have seen them made of wood, clay, Legos, foil, bottle caps, and other things. For some suggestions see pages 90-94 of *Integrating Arts and Crafts in the Jewish School.*

5. **Hanukkah gift wrap and dreidel cutouts.** See pages 99-102 in *Integrating Arts and Crafts in the Jewish School.*

6. **Teach the songs of Hanukkah**

 The New Jewish Songbook by Harry Coopersmith (West Orange, NJ: Behrman House, 1965) contains many Hanukkah songs. A few traditional favorites are "Ma'oz Tzur," "Sivivon," "Mi Y'malel?" "Al Ha-nisim."

 The New Children's Songbook by Velvel Pasternak (Cedarhurst, NY: Tara Publications, 1981) also contains many songs for younger children. Some of these are "Hanerot Halalu," "Ner Li," "I Have a Little Dreidel," "Come Light the Menorah."

7. **Cook potato latkes with your class.**

8. **Do a tzedakah project.** Make sure the needy Jews of your community have hanukkiot and candles for the holiday.

9. **Watch the video *Lights.*** This 30-minute video tells the story of Hanukkah in an entertaining and emotionally moving manner. It is narrated by Judd Hirsch and is available through Ergo Media.

10. **Read the following books to your class:**

 The Hanukkah Story, illustrated book by Marilyn Hirsh (New York: Bonim Books, 1977) tells the Hanukkah story in a historically accurate yet easy-to-understand format. The illustrations are pleasantly accurate.

 The Power of Light. These eight stories by Isaac Bashevis Singer (New York: Farrar, Straus and Giroux, 1980), some set in Europe and some in America, help us to reflect on the Hanukkah experience. They can be read aloud or retold in your own words.

Eight Tales for Eight Nights by Peninnah Schram and Steven Rossman (Northvale, NJ: Jason Aronson, 1990). This collection contains stories from the recollections of these two storytellers.

FAMILY EDUCATION IDEAS ARE LOCATED AT THE END OF THIS GUIDE

TU B'SHEVAT

(Text pages 88-99)

Important Concepts

1. Trees play an important role in our lives.
2. We celebrate the birthday of all trees on the fifteenth day of the Hebrew month Shevat.
3. Jews all over the world help to plant trees in Israel.
4. We celebrate Tu B'Shevat with a special seder meal that features the fruits from trees that grow in Israel.
5. We are the caretakers of God's world.

Background Information

A Personal Experience

I grew up on a stark city street almost entirely devoid of grass and flowers, and especially trees. Yet in front of my house was one glaring exception. There stood a very tall, very wide oak tree. It towered above all the houses on the block and leaned precariously over them. (My parents constantly worried that it would one day fall onto one of the houses during a storm.) It never fell over, but it did capture my childhood imagination.

In 1960 I could not stretch my arms one quarter of the way around my tree. It was at least two hundred years old, so it must have been standing when New York City consisted of just a few blocks near Wall Street and when Native Americans were trading wampum and building outdoor fires for cooking and smoking meat. Horses were probably tied to this tree, and untold numbers of people rested under it. I loved imagining those who had been sheltered by my tree and all that had occurred in its presence. My tree held secrets. It was old and tall and strong, and it protected me.

Trees symbolize many things for us. They express power and strength in their appearance, they symbolize shelter and protection in the way they house birds and insects, and they symbolize historical continuity because they outlive us. From all these concepts comes the Jewish metaphor of the Torah as the "tree of life." Just as the Torah is our strength, our shelter and protection, and our link with the past and future, so are trees. The prayer Etz Chayim states: "The Torah is a tree of life for those who cling to it. Its ways are ways of pleasantness, and all its paths are peace." The value of trees is expressed in the Torah when we are commanded never to destroy an enemy's trees in war. The Jewish calendar provides for a special day to honor trees and the role we play in caring for the earth. The holiday is Tu B'Shevat, the festival of the new year of trees.

An Ancient Holiday for Modern Times

Tu B'Shevat has no particular liturgy and, until recently, was considered a relatively minor holiday. In the late 1800s, however, the agricultural rebirth of the Land of Israel gave Tu B'Shevat a new meaning and new flavor as pioneers reclaimed land damaged by years of overgrazing and erosion.

Today we celebrate Tu B'Shevat by linking ourselves to the Land of Israel. We plant trees through the auspices of the Jewish National Fund, and we eat the fruits of the region. We also use this day as an opportunity to raise ecological issues within the framework of our Jewish lives, and to teach the repairing of the world through conservation and recycling of resources. These two themes—ecology and our connection to the Land of Israel—are the driving themes of this lesson.

Tu B'Shevat has developed into a popular holiday. The creative Tu B'Shevat seder is a full sensory experience of tastes and smells of the Middle East. Figs, dates, nuts, olives, pomegranates, and bokser (St. John's bread), along with an assortment of wines, bring the Israeli sunshine to us during the cold winter. Seder liturgies are available from a variety of sources. If your Temple doesn't offer a Tu B'Shevat seder, by all means start one. It is an excellent family event, enjoyed by people of all ages and easy to prepare and execute.

Introducing the Lesson

Bring to class pictures of various types of trees. You could have one for each child, or simply hold up a few for the group to examine. Ask the children to imagine the tree's location and to guess its approximate age. Ask if the tree seems older or younger than a person. Try to imagine some events that took place during the life of the tree. A discussion should follow of the things that trees provide for us and for other living things, and the fact that some trees can live through several lifetimes of a single human being.

Another way of introducing this lesson is to play "This Is Your Life" as seen on the television show "Sesame Street." Use a puppet of a tree, or even a picture, which you can make talk. You are the game show host, and your puppet is the guest. The tree, who is thrilled to be on television, is introduced one by one to those who played a part in its life: the boy who planted the seed, the girl who watered the tree, the young couple who sat under it, the fisherman who used a branch for his fishing rod, and so on. Each student can take a part. The goal is to find out all the different ways that trees impact on our lives.

At the conclusion, tell the class you are all going to study the Jewish birthday of trees and to learn why we honor trees with a special day.

Teaching the Text

Why Celebrate Trees? Can you think of other ways in which trees help the world?

A Birthday for Trees Discuss how you can determine the approximate age of a tree. How can you tell an old tree from a young tree? Figure out which months on the Gregorian calendar correspond to Shevat. What is the weather like during Tu B'Shevat in the United States? Why is it different from the weather in Israel?

Trees in Israel Explain the concept of erosion and its causes. You can make a mound of sand in a wide, flat, Tupperware container and have children pour water over it in a steady stream. What happens? What if trees were planted on that mound? What would happen to a grassy lawn if a sheep or goat were penned up on it for a month or two?

When to Plant? Show a tree certificate and a blue box from the Jewish National Fund. Explain how we purchase trees and how we can dedicate them in honor or in memory of people we know. How would it feel to have a tree planted for you? How does it feel to plant a tree that we can't see?

A Tu B'Shevat Seder Ask the children to describe a Passover seder. What do we do? What do we eat? Why do we have it? Contrast and compare the Tu B'Shevat seder experience.

Blessing for Fruit and Wine Bring in samples of the different fruits for the class to taste. Point out that figs and dates are plump and juicy when on the tree but are then dried. Explain that this is the same process that is used to make raisins from grapes, and prunes from plums.

Once a man . . . Blessings say thank you to God.

1. Act out how you behave when you are given gifts at your birthday. What do you say? How do you act? How is this similar to the blessings we say to God?

2. Act out being invited to spend the evening at your friend's house. What does your friend give you? What do you give in return?

Planting Partners When we plant, we are acting like God. Plant a tree if you can, or do some indoor planting in small cups or planters. Orange seeds or beans grow quickly and easily. Parsley planted now will be ready to harvest at Passover time.

Let your students act out the story of the old woman and the tree. It can be written out in simple dialogue or ad libbed.

Discuss what it means to do things for the future. Try to list other things we do for which we don't reap the rewards right away. Imagine who planted the trees around your synagogue or home for you.

Taking Care of God's World Participate in an ecology project such as one of the following:

Setting up recycling bins at your synagogue.

Deciding to use the backs of papers before they are tossed out.

Eating on regular dishes instead of using paper plates and cups.

Suggested Activities

1. Plant seeds of your choice indoors in cups or planters.

2. Eat figs, dates, olives, pomegranates, and other Middle Eastern fruit while learning the proper blessing.

3. Write the blessing for fruit on top of a page and have the students color or cut and paste various fruits to illustrate it.

4. The Jewish National Fund offers free material on all levels for Tu B'Shevat. They can be reached at:

> Jewish National Fund
> Department of Education
> 114 East 32nd Street
> New York, NY 10016

5. Make a large paper tree and put a picture of each student on the branches. You can also attach to the branches paper fruits that the children have made.

6. Compare the American legend of Johnny Appleseed to the story of the Old Woman and the Tree.

7. Plant a tree on the synagogue grounds if possible.

8. Collect money to plant trees in Israel.

9. Create your own tree. Stick a lump of clay to a square of cardboard. Find an interesting twig and stand it in the clay. Decorate it with paper leaves, a kite, and other materials.

PURIM

(Text pages 100-115)

Important Concepts

1. Purim is a carnival holiday when we dress in costumes, act silly, and play games.

2. On Purim we read Megillat Esther, the story of beautiful Queen Esther and wicked Haman. We read how Esther saved the Jewish people from the plot of wicked Haman and how Esther, with the help of her cousin Mordecai, rose above her fears to save her people.

3. As we read the Megillah, we drown out the sound of Haman's name with noisemakers called graggers. Doing this reminds us that it is our duty to stamp out hatred when we see or hear it.

4. We eat a special Purim cookie called *hamantashen*.

5. We send gifts of fruit and cookies to our friends and to the poor. These are called *mishloah manot*.

6. The Purim story teaches us that we must have courage to help others in times of trouble.

Vocabulary

Adar The sixth month of the Jewish year. Adar is a leap month, so in nine out of every seventeen years there are two months of Adar. Purim occurs on the 14th of Adar. If there are two months of Adar, Purim occurs in the second Adar.

Ahasuerus According to the Book of Esther, the King of Persia. None of the known records of the Persian empire contain this name.

Esther The Jewish queen of Persia who risked her life to save her fellow Jews. She is a symbol of courage and heroism for Jews everywhere.

Gragger The Yiddish word for noisemaker. We use graggers to drown out the name of Haman during the reading of the megillah. The Hebrew word for gragger is *ra'ashan*.

Haman The evil advisor of King Ahasuerus who wants to kill all the Jews.

71

Hamantashen In Yiddish, these sweet triangular cookies are known as "Haman's hat." They are filled with fruit and eaten on Purim. In Hebrew they are known as *oznai Haman* or "Haman's ears."

Megillah A megillah is a scroll. We read the Book of Esther aloud in the synagogue from a scroll. On other holidays, we read other megillot. For example, we read the Book of Ruth on Shavuot, Song of Songs on Passover, and Ecclesiastes on Sukkot.

Mishloah manot Baskets of cookies and fruit that we send to friends and family on Purim. We also make baskets for the poor and for those who might not be able to come to synagogue.

Mordecai Queen Esther's uncle who encouraged Esther to save the Jews of Persia.

Purim The word *purim* refers to the lots or dice that Haman used to determine the day that he would kill the Jews of Persia.

Background Information

A Personal Experience

Several years ago, as a part of a Sunday morning lesson, I thought I would tell the Purim story to my class of first graders. I proceeded to launch into the tale of Mordecai, Haman, King Ahasuerus, Vashti, and Esther with gusto, but within seconds I found my audience staring at me with very confused faces. I had become bogged down in twists of plot, palace intrigue, and sexual innuendo, and I realized then that this story does not read like a modern children's tale.

True to the tradition of the ancient Persian world, the Megillat Esther reads like a tale from the *Thousand and One Arabian Nights*. The plot twists and turns like the catacombs of the ancient kings. There is a lot of "Meanwhile, back at the palace . . ." and all this makes the story a bit hard to follow at first. On a second hearing, however, it is a wonderful glimpse into the palace life of Persia: harems, monarchs, and more. The characters are serious as well as funny, fictional in some ways and disturbingly true in others. The story of Esther offers us caricatures of personality types: the evil vizier, the young and beautiful queen, the foolish monarch. Yet they are also Hitler, Hannah Senesh, and perhaps King Hussein.

The wonderful thing about Purim is that we can take all the serious aspects of our history and for one day conquer them with laughter and frivolity. We drown out the sound of Haman's name, we cheer brave Esther and Mordecai, we laugh at foolish King

Ahasuerus, all to make the world, for that one day, just as it should be. Evil is successfully silenced, an anti-feminist king is forced to listen to his wife in order to undo his own stupidity, and good not only wins but is offered power and position as reward. For that one day, life is as it ought to be.

How Purim Began

The feast of Purim occurs on the 14th day of the Hebrew month Adar (except in walled cities such as Jerusalem, where it is celebrated on the 15th). Purim arrives as the winter cold is beginning to break and the first buds of spring are beginning to appear. It is a time of release, of breaking free from the constraints of winter. We create a carnival atmosphere where bending the rules is acceptable. It is serious as well as fun, for we also read the Book of Esther, whose themes of unity and courage give cause for reflection.

Purim probably has its origins in the emulation of a Persian spring feast day. Some feel that the story of Esther was written as a historical novel during the Maccabean period. The story was thus intended to comment on the dangers of Jews living under Greek rule. During this time, another holiday was celebrated during Adar. It was Nicanor Day, a commemoration of the defeat of Antiochus' general Nicanor by the Maccabees. That fast day, mentioned in the Talmud, is no longer celebrated. Perhaps the rabbis of the Talmud, who were opposed to the glorification of the Maccabees, preferred Esther and Haman, who defeated evil without any mention of the Maccabees. At any rate, Purim is given much space in the Mishnah, while Nicanor Day is only mentioned.

Celebrating Purim

Purim seems always to have been celebrated with frivolity. The details of just how we celebrate probably evolved over time. The Italian Jews of the fifteenth century were taken by the Mardi Gras festival in spring and incorporated many of the customs of Mardi Gras into Purim. Dressing up was a significant aspect of the celebration, and we can therefore guess that the custom of wearing costumes comes from this time.

Since Purim is not a religious festival there are no work prohibitions. On Purim we are free to be foolish. We dress in costumes, design silly pranks, play games, make noise. Respected members of the community appear as Flipper or Spiderman, telling jokes and accepting barbs. (One year in our synagogue a group of teens dressed as the rabbi, playing the part to a tee.) On Purim the rules are abandoned—anything goes. There is a Hebrew saying, "*Kol yom lo Purim*," "Every day is not Purim." We use it during the year when someone is acting too silly, is out of line, or is excessive in poking fun at someone else, adult as well as child.

The day before Purim is known as the Fast of Esther. Traditional Jews fast from dawn to dusk on this day, although this practice is commonly avoided through the study of Talmud on that day: When one celebrates the mitzvah of Torah study, it is permissible to override the mitzvah to fast. It is interesting to note that among the *Conversos* of Spain, those forced to convert to Christianity, the Fast of Esther was kept throughout the generations on an equal par with Yom Kippur, even when the meaning of the fast became lost. There are places in Portugal today where Purim is remembered as the Feast of Saint Esther even though the Catholic celebrants are unaware of any Jewish connection.

We read the entire Megillah on both the evening and the morning of Purim. Every time the name of Haman is spoken we drown it out. Children use graggers (*ra'ashanim* in Hebrew) for the task.

There is a custom of sharing baskets of treats with friends and with the poor. These baskets are known as *mishloah manot,* which means "sending gifts." In Jewish neighborhoods, children walk from door to door delivering their cookies and fruits. Usually, however, we use the synagogue as a meeting place for the sharing and distribution of these treats.

The cookies that traditionally fill these baskets are known as *hamantashen* (Haman's hat), or *oznai Haman* (Haman's ears). They are triangular in shape and contain fruit filling.

Other customs for Purim include the "Purim Rabbi." Released for a day from the "yoke of the Torah," the rabbi is free to satirize his role, as well as the sacred texts. It is traditional in many synagogues for the rabbi to give his own *shpiel* during the Purim service. (A "Purimspiel," or *shpiel*, is a satirical skit or other type of presentation.) Some communities prepare a special Purim *shpiel* to present to the group. It can revolve around the Book of Esther or any other topic that the group chooses. It is common to satirize people and situations that are familiar to all.

Introducing the Lesson

If your students are like mine, they love to dress up. Children find it very easy to slip into the role of Batman or Superman, Peter Pan or Wendy. They enjoy spending the afternoon being someone else.

Begin class by asking your students what costumes they have at home, or who they like to pretend to be. You might ask them to complete the following sentence.

"When I play, I like to pretend to be _____."

Spend a few minutes letting all the students express themselves. Ask them why they like to be that character.

Explain to the class that we have a special holiday called Purim when everyone gets to dress up as his or her favorite character. They can even go to synagogue in costume. Explain that the Purim story has special characters and that you are about to learn that story. Tell them that after reading the story, they might decide to be one of these characters. They can choose from (here you might outline the characters in an enticing way):

The evil Haman

The beautiful and brave Queen Esther

The brave and intelligent Mordecai

The foolish King Ahasuerus

The proud and independent Vashti

Let's find out who these characters are and what they did!

Teaching the Story

The Purim story is slightly longer and more complex than the average children's story. Here are some suggestions for making the story fun and understandable.

Set the scene. Explain that ancient Persia is now modern Iran. Try to show some pictures of the type of artwork, architecture, clothing, or food that is common in the area. To show the style of dress, a simple source might be a picture book of *Aladdin and His Lamp*. Talk about some of the ways that life was different then. Point out that there was a king who had a special advisor to help him make important decisions. Explain to your class that women could not choose their husbands and that they had very little say in the daily goings on of life.

Go through the story with actors and costumes. Create a special hat for each of the main characters and assign a student to play each part. As the class reads through the story, refer to these actors as their parts come up.

Discuss the characters. Make a chart that lists the main characters across the top. Discuss their attributes and have the class list them under each name. An example might be:

ESTHER
beautiful
shy
courageous

Discuss the ways in which this story is similar to the Hanukkah story. (It involves Jews as a minority living under oppressive rule. In each case, one special Jew rises up to save his or her people from destruction.)

Discuss other people in Jewish history who are like the characters in the Purim story.

Haman—Amalek, Hitler

Esther—Hannah Senesh, Golda Meir

Have the children write a brief essay on who they feel is their favorite character and why. You can also do the same project asking children to choose their favorite scene.

Discuss the lessons that we can learn from the Purim story. Examples are:

It is important to be brave.

It is important to care about others.

It is important to feel a special bond with other Jewish people.

Sometimes we need to overcome our fears in order to do what is right. We must work for justice in our world.

Sometimes we need to break the rules if doing so will accomplish an important goal.

Teaching the Text

The Megillah Reading A megillah is a scroll. You might want to point out to your students that in ancient times every book was in the form of a scroll. A library in those days was filled with shelves of scrolls.

Whenever we hear Haman's name . . . We wish to drown out the sound of Haman's name. In the same way, a scribe crosses out the name of Amalek as a part of his preparation for writing a Torah.

Purim is a noisy, jolly holiday . . . It is traditional to dress up as one of the Purim characters, though any costume is fine. Engage the children in a discussion of what they will dress up as on Purim.

Hamantashen Hamantashen cookies are shaped like Haman's hat. At this point you might want to teach the song, "My Hat It Has Three Corners." We sing it on Purim because it reminds us of Haman's hat. It can be sung in Hebrew or English and has hand signs to go along with the words. The English words are as follows:

My hat it has three corners, three corners has my hat.

And had it not three corners, it would not be my hat.

The hand signs are as follows: When you say "my," point to yourself. When you say "hat," point to your head. On the word "three," hold up three fingers. When you say "corners," make a triangle with your fingers. As you sing the song, you can replace the sung word with the appropriate hand sign. On each repetition, replace one additional sung word until all of the hand signs are being used.

Mishloah Manot Discuss who your class might wish to give baskets to.

The Purim story gives us courage . . . Ask the class what they think the story teaches. Ask, "What can we learn from the way Esther behaved? What can we learn from the way Mordecai behaved? In similar situations, how should we behave?"

Suggested Activities

1. Have your students act out a simple version of the Purim story. You might wish to use simple props and costumes to help the students be as expressive as possible.

2. Make Purim puppets. Paper bag puppets are simple and fun. So are popsicle stick puppets. You can create a character on a toilet paper roll and glue a popsicle stick to the base. The child can hold the stick and move the puppet. For other puppet ideas see *Integrating Arts and Crafts in the Jewish School*, pages 128-133.

3. Make Purim masks. For ideas see *Integrating Arts and Crafts in the Jewish School*, pages 122-127.

4. Make your own megillah. Use a long strip of paper with an unsharpened pencil attached to each end. Roll the paper around the pencils. Decorate the paper with scenes from the Purim story. Use key phrases and write the names of the characters in both Hebrew and English.

5. Make a mural depicting the Purim story.

6. Make graggers. Any noisemaker will do, but there are some suggestions on pages 136-141 of *Integrating Arts and Crafts in the Jewish School*.

7. Bake hamantashen with your class. I always find that this project works best if the dough is prepared ahead of time. The students need only roll each circle of dough, add the filling, and pinch it together. Then the cookies can all be baked at once.

8. Make mishloah manot baskets. Have the children bring in treats such as raisins, candy, and the like. Use the hamantashen that you baked plus the added treats to put together baskets for the poor or for members of the congregation who are in nursing homes. You can conclude the project by taking the children to deliver the baskets in person.

9. Create pictures made from words. A traditional form of Jewish art is to make pictures out of the text that relates to the theme of your picture. I have a wall hanging of

Esther that is made out of the text of the Megillah. For children, you might ask them to draw a picture of Esther that is made out of her name, or a picture of Haman made out of his name. You may write the name in any form you like and repeat it as many times as you like.

10. **Books for Purim.** There are many books on this holiday, but here are a couple: *Cakes And Miracles* by Barbara Goldin (New York: Viking Press, 1991) and *Here Come the Purim Players* by B. Cohen and B. Brodsky (New York: Lothrop, Lee and Shepard).

11. **Songs for Purim.** There are many fun songs for Purim. Some can be found in *The New Children's Songbook* by Velvel Pasternak (Cedarhurst, NY: Tara Publications, 1981, pages 28-32). *The New Jewish Songbook* by Harry Coopersmith (West Orange, NJ: Behrman House, 1965) includes "Hag Purim" and "Utsu Etsa." "Vashti's Song" by Debbie Friedman can be found on the tape *Debbie Friedman Live* (Sounds Write Productions, 1990). It is a funny look at the Purim story through the eyes of the woman who loses her position at the very beginning of the tale.

FAMILY EDUCATION IDEAS ARE LOCATED AT THE END OF THIS GUIDE

PASSOVER

(Text pages 116-133)

Important Concepts

1. On Passover we remember that we were once slaves in Egypt but that with the help of God and the guidance of Moses we were led to freedom.

2. One of the reasons we remember these events of our past is so that we will treat those in need with kindness and respect.

3. We reread the story of Passover each year at the seder from a book called the Haggadah.

4. At the seder, the youngest child who is able to recites the four questions.

5. We place a special plate on the seder table that holds the symbolic foods of the holiday.

6. We invite special guests to our seder.

7. We drink four cups of wine.

8. Passover is a time when we remember the Prophet Elijah.

9. We hunt for the afikoman at the Passover seder.

10. During the week of Passover we eat matzah instead of bread.

Vocabulary

Afikoman This refers to the middle matzah of the three placed on the seder table. The word comes from Greek and is thought to mean "dessert." The meal can't be concluded without the afikoman, so children often steal and hide it during the meal to hold it for ransom.

Cup of Elijah Elijah the prophet is said to visit each home during Passover. We set a special cup of wine out for him in anticipation of his visit. Elijah will herald the coming of the Messianic Age, which tradition says may very well begin on Passover.

Four Questions This section of the Haggadah, read by the youngest child, sets the tone for the seder: an opportunity to teach our children the events of our past.

Haggadah The Hebrew word for "telling," the Haggadah is the text from which we read during the seder. Canonized sometime during the Middle Ages, this book offers tales and commentary as well as songs and liturgy for the celebration of Passover.

Hametz This is the Hebrew word for "leaven." We do not eat any foods on Passover that are hametz, or that have risen. These include wheat, barley, spelt, oats, rye, and corn. Some people include rice, peas, and beans in this group.

Haroset A mixture of chopped nuts, wine, and apples that reminds us of the mortar Jewish slaves used to make bricks. Sephardic Jews use dates and raisins to make their haroset.

Maror Bitter herbs which remind us of the bitterness of slavery. Horseradish is often used for maror.

Matzah Flat bread that we eat during the week of Passover. It is made in less than 18 minutes so that it is given no opportunity to rise. Matzah reminds us of our ancestors' quick flight from slavery.

Moses The leader of the Jewish people who was chosen by God to lead us out of slavery.

Pharaoh The ruler of Egypt at the time of the Exodus. Pharaoh is a title rather than a name, and there were many Pharaohs who ruled Egypt over the years. Some were accepting of the Jewish people, although this Pharaoh was not.

Seder The Hebrew word for "order." It refers to the order of the Passover rituals on the first and second evening of the holiday. We get together with family and friends to feast, sing, and tell the story of the Exodus.

Ten Plagues The ten terrible events that God inflicted upon the Pharaoh because he would not free the Jewish people. The plagues are listed in the Haggadah.

Background Information

A Personal Experience

For me, Passover is the most emotionally charged of all the Jewish holidays. The intensity of the preparations, the cleaning, shopping, and cooking, the discarding of all that is old and ragged, the bringing out of all that is fresh and new, all serve to heighten the experience. The sight of the special Passover dishes, the fancy once-a-year tablecloth, the removal of Elijah's cup from its place on the shelf to its perch in the center of the table, the taste of haroset as it is chopped, the smell of matzah ball soup, all create subconscious connections to Passovers of years past.

We bring out extra tables, prepare for guests who are coming from a distance, dust off the Haggadot with their beautiful pictures of Moses and Pharaoh and the parting of the sea. We search for hametz, then build a backyard fire to burn the remains, feeling purified and free as the weeks of cleaning come to a close.

I am grateful for the repetition of this ritual year after year, for the children in clean shirts and dresses sliding into their assigned places, for the reading of the Haggadah parts that have developed ownership over time, for my daughter's voice as she sings the four questions, and for my husband who sings "Had Gadya" in one breath as my father had done when I was young.

There is that first taste of matzah, the inevitable commentary on the matzah balls (too soft or too hard), plots to steal the afikoman, my father-in-law's argument on some point from the Haggadah, and last but not least, my mother-in-law's rendition of "Let My People Go."

As Passover comes each year, we relive those old memories and create new ones. Our family and friends merge with us and with the whole Jewish world to celebrate our redemption from bondage. With one voice we proclaim, "We were slaves in Egypt," and we are transported back to those very days when the sea parted for us all. And although we come from all walks of life and disagree on many issues, we stand together on this night as the door is opened for Elijah, each hoping in his or her own way that this will be the year he appears—"May he come speedily in our own day."

A Historical Perspective

Jacob and his sons followed Joseph down to Egypt during a time of famine. They lived and prospered in Egypt for many years until political changes made the climate less hospitable for Jews. A Pharaoh arose "who knew not Joseph" and used the Jews as slaves to build projects for the Egyptian empire. Life became even more unbearable as Pharaoh decreed that every firstborn Jew would be thrown into the Nile. After much effort to secure the Pharaoh's permission to leave Egypt, God led us out with "a mighty hand and an outstretched arm." The sea parted, and we became free to remember and celebrate forever the event.

The Torah tells us, "You shall observe the Feast of Unleavened Bread for on this very day I brought your ranks out of the land of Egypt; you shall observe this day throughout the generations as an institution for all time. In the first month, from the fourteenth day of the month at evening, you shall eat unleavened bread until the twenty-first day of the month at evening" (Exodus 12:17-18). So the Torah itself proclaims this festival, letting us know that the celebration of this holiday dates from very early times.

Scholars feel that there were originally two festivals. One was an agricultural festival called *Hag HaMatzot*, celebrated by farmers. Farmers made a special effort at this time of year to clean the previous year's grain out their storehouses, because the barley harvest was about to begin and the old grain in the bins would spoil the new grain. The second festival, celebrated by shepherds, was *Hag HaPesah*, or festival of the Paschal Lamb. A special lamb was sacrificed at this time of year, and its blood was smeared on the doorposts of the tents. These two holidays eventually merged into our present-day festival of deliverance. The matzah became the symbol of haste in the wilderness, and the lamb blood became the sign to God to pass over the Jewish houses on the night of the tenth plague. The sacrifice of the lamb was discontinued with the destruction of the Temple in 70 C.E., although the Samaritans in Israel still follow the Torah literally on this point.

Passover has been widely celebrated since earliest times. Josephus, the well-known historian of the Second Temple period, described Passover celebrations in Jerusalem. He told of approximately three million people pouring into the city for the festival, each family group with a sacrificial lamb. Families would come to Jerusalem (for Passover is one of the three pilgrimage festivals), stay the week, and visit with family and friends while feasting on the lamb.

The Mishnah gives us much information on how to celebrate the festival. This is where the original interpretations of the Passover symbols come from. "The lamb is offered because God passed over, the unleavened bread is eaten because God redeemed the Israelites from Egypt [Exodus 12:39], and the bitter herbs because the Egyptians embittered their lives. [Exodus 1:14] (Pesahim 10:5)."

Passover is celebrated for eight days, seven days among Reform Jews. We refrain from work on the first two and the last two days. The seder is celebrated on the first two evenings. In Israel the holiday is seven days, with a seder on the first day only. The last day is reserved for saying Yizkor. The Jews of North Africa celebrate the *maimuna* on the last day; this is a large hametz party. In the United States we might informally go out for pizza after the week of abstinence, but North African Jews have a formal feast to mark the end of the hametz fast.

Preparing for Passover

Preparations for Passover are detailed and complex. We rid our homes and belongings of all grain products: wheat, barley, spelt, oats, rye, and (since 1492) corn. (Rice, peas, and beans were added to the list by the Jews of Eastern Europe, although Jews of the Middle East do not ban these foods.) Alcohol made from grains and grain vinegars are also removed. These foods are packed into boxes and often given to the local food bank.

When the house is clean, we change our dishes and cooking utensils for the week of Passover. On the final evening before the holiday we hunt for the last crumbs of hametz. Some like to do this in the traditional manner, with candle and feather, looking under every bed to be sure all has been removed. The next morning a fire is made outdoors to burn the last crumbs. Some people like to fast on the day of the seder so that the first taste of matzah is fresh and special. Even if you don't fast, you are supposed to refrain from eating matzah before the seder.

The Seder

The seder is performed in the evening. Family, friends, and special guests arrive for the event. There is a special stress on hospitality this evening. Many try to invite those who have no place to celebrate.

The seder is described in detail in the Haggadah. The Haggadah explains all the ritual objects, offers us background and midrashim on the events we are to remember, offers us prayers and blessings, and has lots of songs. It is designed with children in mind, with special songs and parts designed to keep children active and awake, for the seder can go on until midnight. We retell the Exodus so that we can inform our children of these events. Each year we want to feel as though we ourselves are leaving Egypt. Some Oriental Jews take this idea even further by actually acting out the Exodus during the seder.

What Happens at the Seder?

The Haggadah was codified in the Middle Ages. Although there are many different Haggadot to choose from, the basic elements of each are the same. The service covers four basic themes: our slavery, giving thanks for our freedom, the rebirth of spring, and a look toward the future in the sections on Elijah the Prophet. We place a special ceremonial plate on the table with five symbolic foods on it: a roasted egg to symbolize spring; a roasted bone to remind us of the Passover sacrifice of Temple days; bitter herbs to remind us of the bitterness of slavery; haroset, the mix of apples and nuts that reminds us of the mortar that was used to build with bricks; and parsley, to remind us of spring. We dip the parsley in salted water that simulates the tears of our oppression. We also drink four cups of wine, each to remind us of one of the four expressions of our redemption in Exodus 6:6-7. Some scholars feel that the four cups of wine were added as an emulation of the Roman banquets. Our custom of reclining was also left to us from the Romans, who always reclined on sofas while eating.

At the beginning of the seder the youngest child recites the four questions. We then read about the four types of children and how they all need to be taught about the Exodus. We recite the Ten Plagues, placing one drop of wine on our plates for each plague. We sing "Dayenu," explain the meaning of the Passover symbols aloud, and then eat them. We praise God and sing some more. The meal is large and sumptuous, the wine sweet, the company exceptional.

During the meal, the afikoman—the middle matzah from the ceremonial matzah plate—is broken in half. The leader lifts the afikoman and states that this is the dessert and that the seder cannot conclude until it is eaten. This is the cue for someone to steal and hide the afikoman so that at the end of the meal it must be ransomed back from the children in order for the meal to conclude. It is customary to offer cash or small gifts for those who return the afikoman.

Throughout the seder, the theme of the holiday remains in focus: We were once slaves, and now we are free. How lucky we are. May we always remember that not all people are free and that it is our responsibility to help them in any way we can.

We are a people with a past, a history that we share. We left Egypt together and, like any people who share an adventure, we are closely bonded by it.

We are a people with a future. We wait for Elijah each year with courage and faith that one day the world will indeed be cured of its ills. We place Elijah's cup on the table knowing that we can work to make it happen. And as we recite "Next year in Jerusalem" at the end of the seder, we look forward to the new year, feeling optimistic, enthusiastic, and full!

Introducing the Lesson

Ask your students to answer the following question: "If you had to teach some important information, such as the life of Abraham Lincoln, or what Thanksgiving is all about, how would you teach it so that your students would remember the information?" Have the children compile a list of the things they would do to teach these facts. It might look as follows:

1. Describe the information.
2. Sing a song about it.
3. Ask the students questions.
4. Read a book about it.
5. Look at pictures about it.
6. Act out the story.

Explain that that is what Passover is all about. Parents teach, learn, and remember what happened to the Jewish people in Egypt many years ago. We also teach our children by having a Passover seder. At the seder we tell the Passover story, sing, ask questions, and eat the foods that teach us what happened long ago.

Teaching the Story

The Passover Story Discuss what it means to be a slave. If we were slaves, how would our lives be different? What would it feel like?

But one baby boy was saved . . . Discuss how Moses' mother felt when she heard that all the Jewish baby boys were to be drowned. How did she feel when she put Moses in the basket?

An Egyptian princess found him . . . Tell your class about Moses' sister, Miriam, who watched Moses in the basket from the rushes. When Miriam saw the Pharaoh's daughter pick up the baby, Miriam suggested to Pharaoh's daughter that Moses' mother be the nurse for the baby.

When Moses was a grown man . . . Why did God choose to speak to Moses through the symbol of the burning bush? (God is never fully revealed. A bush that does not burn up is a supernatural event that demonstrates God's presence.)

There was no way to escape . . . A story from the midrash goes as follows: The Jews stood at the shores of the sea. Nothing happened until one man, Nachshon Ben Aminadav, took the initiative of wading into the water. He waded all the way up to his neck, and when it looked like he was about to drown, God parted the sea, and all the people followed. This story shows that we crossed to safety with God's help, but that a human was also needed to take the first step.

At the end of the story you might want to teach the Hebrew words for a slave (*eved*) and a free person (*ben horin*).

Teaching the Text

The Seder Stress that we all experience the events of the Exodus as if we had been the ones who left Egypt. The seder is a retelling to remind us of these events from long ago. Oriental Jews get up from the seder table and act out the Exodus with costumes and props. Perhaps your students would like to do the same.

The Four Questions At Passover, children ask the questions to show that the retelling of the Passover story is for them. Practice singing the four questions. Point out that it is really one question with four statements. Discuss each statement as you learn it.

Why Do We Eat Matzah? Have matzah on hand to offer a taste during the lesson. Discuss how eating special foods can help us to remember what life was like so long ago.

Inviting Guests Ask the students to tell whom they invite to their Passover seder.

The Four Cups of Wine You might want to have some sweet wine or grape juice on hand for a taste during this part of the lesson.

The Cup of Elijah Show a Cup of Elijah. Sing "Eliyahu Hanavi" and discuss what the words mean.

The Seder Plate Show each of the five foods that go on the seder plate. Discuss the significance of each one. Make a seder plate art project that shows each food and explains its meaning.

Why Do We Recline? This custom entered Jewish life during our contact with the Romans. The Romans reclined on sofas at every feast or banquet.

Afikoman Describe the custom of having an adult hide the afikoman, or having the child steal the afikoman, in order to have it ransomed back at the end of the meal. The meal is not supposed to end without the afikoman, which comes from the middle matzah on the ceremonial plate.

Suggested Activities

1. **Act out sections of the Passover story.** Use simple props and costumes such as hats, a staff, and so on. Discuss important points as you go along.

2. **Make a Haggadah.** Give each child a booklet of construction paper that is stapled at the binding. Select the important sections and have the children paste in small prepared sections of the text. Key words and the blessings can be in Hebrew. Have the children then illustrate their work. Make sure the book moves from right to left.

3. **Illustrate scenes from the Passover story individually or as a mural.**

4. **Make Passover cards or seder invitations.** Have the children learn to write the words "seder" and "Pesah" in Hebrew.

5. **Have a "Memorize the Plagues" contest.** Offer small prizes to the children who can recite them unaided.

6. **Make a matzah factory.** Mix flour and water until it can be kneaded easily. Knead and roll the dough into thin sheets. Punch with a fork and bake in a hot oven until slightly

brown. For the matzah to be kosher, the whole process must take under eighteen minutes so the dough has no chance to rise. Use a timer for fun.

7. **Make an illustrated chart of foods we can and can't eat on Passover.**

8. **Act out the search for leaven,** *B'dekat Hametz*, **with candles and a feather.** Hide pieces of bread around the room, and have the children find them. You can also hide packaged food items that are hametz, and after they are found donate them to the local food bank.

9. **Discuss the four children of the Haggadah.** Describe what each one is like and why they need to be taught in different ways. Ask which one each child would like to be.

10. **Sing songs and blessings.** There is so much music for Passover, but this list is a beginning:

"Eliahu Hanavi," "Adir Hu," "Ehad Mi Yodeah," "Dayenu," "Let My People Go," "Had Gadya" (also in English), "B'Chol Dor VaDor," "L'Shanah HaBa'a," "Mah Nishtanah" (The Four Questions).

Many Haggadot have song sections in the back. Most Jewish music books also have Passover sections that contain many of these songs.

FAMILY EDUCATION IDEAS ARE LOCATED AT THE END OF THIS GUIDE

YOM HASHOAH

(Text pages 134-135)

Shoah is the Hebrew word for "Holocaust." Both in Hebrew and in English it is an uncompromising word that depicts the terror of its reality.

I am old enough to have personally known many survivors. Members of my own family, parents of friends that I grew up with, both touched me in silent ways, communicating their tragedies to me in small but poignant gestures. I have often wondered about the family friends I never had the opportunity to know, the aunt I was named after, the "first family" of my best friend's mother. They are always with me, but I wonder if they will be with my children. They too have known survivors, but not as closely as I have. They read *Anne Frank, Number the Stars, Maus,* and the books of Elie Wiesel. Yet with each day, the distance grows and the challenge of remembering becomes greater.

That is where we, the teachers, come in, for it is our responsibility to aid this process of remembering. Just as we recall the Maccabees, the Exodus from Egypt, the revelation at Sinai, so too we must teach the Holocaust, although this is a more delicate task, especially with young children. How can we teach the Holocaust experience without unduly frightening the child?

When I was a child I always loved to ask my father, "What was it like in Poland when you were a child?" And after stories of the big black stove in the kitchen, of the runaway horse and cart that he lost control of when he was seven, there would come the inevitable end of the story: "No one from that town is left. They all died in the war." This frightened me as a child, and my father knew that, so he lied to me, a sweet and loving lie that I thought was true well into my adulthood. "Don't worry," he would tell me. "There are more Jews alive today than there were before the war." But despite his reassurance, Hitler chased me in my dreams for many years.

Rather than tell those well-meaning lies, we have several good books available to help teach the Holocaust experience to young children. *Promise of a New Spring* by Gerda Klein (Dallas: Rossel Books, 1981), *The Number on My Grandfather's Arm* by David Adler (New York: U.A.H.C., 1987), and *Terrible Things* by Eve Bunting (Philadelphia: Jewish

Publication Society, 1989) all tell stories that a child can understand and relate to without feeling overwhelmed.

You might want to show your class a yahrzeit candle. Discuss its use, when we light it, and why. You might also want to teach the Kaddish prayer, or just recite it, pointing out that the words are an affirmation of life. Discuss why we affirm life when we are thinking most about death.

An appropriate song to teach during this lesson would be "Ani Ma'amin." The words translate, "I believe with perfect faith, that even though the Messiah tarries, the Messiah will one day come."

YOM HA'ATZMA'UT

(Text pages 136-147)

Important Concepts

1. Yom Ha'atzma'ut is the birthday of the State of Israel. It occurs on the fifth of Iyar.
2. The modern state of Israel was born in 1948.
3. Even though we were forced to leave the Land of Israel two thousand years ago, we have always remembered our homeland.
4. Theodor Herzl is the father of modern Zionism.
5. The Jews of Israel had to fight to make Israel a Jewish country.
6. Jews come to live in Israel from all over the world.
7. Hebrew is the language spoken in Israel.

Vocabulary

Aliyah The word *aliyah* means "going up." We use the phrase "making aliyah" to refer to the act of going to live in Israel, because we see this as a spiritual ascent. In the same way, we see the act of being called to the Torah to say the blessing (which is referred to as "having an aliyah") as a spiritual ascent.

Hatikvah *Hatikvah* is the Hebrew word for "hope." It is also the name of the national anthem of Israel.

Theodor Herzl A journalist from Vienna who encouraged Jews to resettle the land of Israel and create a national homeland. His ideas of statehood for the Jewish people became known as "Zionism," and he is now known as the father of modern Zionism.

Hora A joyous Israeli dance performed in a circle. The hora has become a common form of celebration in the streets of Israel on holidays.

Kibbutzim The root of the word *kibbutz* means "draw together." A kibbutz is a community of people who work and live together, sharing common goals and the profits of their labor.

Kotel The word *kotel* means "wall." This specific wall is the last remaining outer stone wall of the ancient Temple that stood in Jerusalem before it was destroyed by the Romans in 70 C.E. Today it is a holy site where people come to pray.

Magen David This is the six-pointed star found on the Israeli flag. A *magen* is a "shield." The star is traditionally known as the symbol that adorned David's shield.

Medinat Yisrael Hebrew for "the State of Israel."

Ulpan An *ulpan* is literally a studio or place where one thing is done intensively. We commonly use this word to mean a school that teaches intensive Hebrew to new Israeli immigrants.

Zionism A belief that arose in Europe in the late 1800s that the Jewish people need to be responsible for their own destiny through living in and running their own sovereign state.

Background Information

A Personal Experience

Recently I was teaching a group of Bar/Bat Mitzvah students the proper choreography for the recitation of the Amidah prayer. It is customary when reciting this prayer to rise, face east, and take three steps forward before beginning. I asked the group why we do these things. No one knew, so I explained. "We rise because this is the most important prayer. We recite it as though we are entering God's presence. We face east so that we are facing Jerusalem, our holy city, and we take three steps forward in order to express the feeling of entering the throne room of the Holy One. At the end of the prayer," I added, "we take three steps back again in order to signify our leaving."

We practiced doing this a few times. The following week when we met for our lesson, I asked if anyone remembered why we do these three things. They remembered why we rise, and they remembered why we face east, but there was silence when I asked about taking the three steps. After a quiet moment of shifting around, one brave girl spoke up. "We take three steps forward because we really want to go to Israel," she guessed, "and when we know that we really can't go there today, then we take three steps back."

Oh, well. Even the best students don't always remember all the information, but I thought this response was rather interesting. Embedded in the Jewish psyche is our connection to the Land of Israel. Even though it was not exactly the correct response, this girl knew that we express our feelings toward our homeland through our prayer, and even though she wasn't sure exactly how, she made a logical, Jewish guess.

For over two thousand years we have maintained our connection to the Land of Israel, mainly through our thoughts and prayers. When we end the Passover seder, we sing, "Next Year in Jerusalem." When we recite the Birkat Hamazon, we ask God to rebuild Jerusalem speedily. A standard synagogue service includes a prayer for the State of Israel, and we teach all our young people to sing "Hatikvah." As adults we join Zionist organizations such as Hadassah and give our tzedakah money to United Jewish Appeal or to Jewish National Fund, the organization that plants trees in Israel.

Many of us who were born after 1948 have trouble imagining a world without an Israel. Israel has always been there for us, making deserts bloom, defeating enemies despite all odds, showing a face of Jewish strength in the world. And yet, for two thousand years before this, there was no Jewish state, and life was very different for the Jewish people. In the face of oppression and intolerance there was nowhere to turn. Those days are easy to forget in the short time since 1948, and one of the most important things we can communicate to our students is to not take Israel for granted. We must teach that the State of Israel needs the support of world Jewry, for the country sits in what seems to be a permanently fragile situation.

We must encourage future American Jews to give to UJA, to plant trees, to spend a year of high school or college studying in Israel. We must teach them how beautiful our land is and how much we need it.

"If you will it, it is no dream." Theodor Herzl called Jews to action with these famous words at the First Zionist Congress. We are the inheritors of these beautiful words even today as we bring Russians and Ethiopians home to Israel for better lives as free Jews. So as players in the drama that is Israel's story, we continue to act. The book is not closed; we just need to write the next chapter.

A Historical Perspective

Joshua brought the Jews into the land of Israel in about 1200 B.C.E. The kings of Israel—Saul, David, Solomon, and others—ruled for about a thousand years until the destruction of the Second Temple by the Romans in 70 C.E. At that time Rome removed Israel's status as a province of the Roman Empire and attached the little strip of land to Syria. Except for a brief period during the Bar Kochba rebellion, Jews did not rule the Land of Israel again until 1948.

Throughout two thousand years of exile there were always Jews that remained in the land of Israel. Every generation brought pilgrims who settled in the land, and there

94

were often scholars who went there to study. But the Jews remained poor and few in number, often dependent on the help of world Jewry for their survival.

Zionism

During the nineteenth century some European Jews began to call for a return to Israel. They called themselves Zionists after the term "Zion," the tall hill in the center of the city of Jerusalem. Wealthy European Jews such as the Rothschilds began buying up tracts of land for agricultural settlements, and Jews began to resettle the land. The city of Tel Aviv was founded in 1909 when Arabs refused to let Jews settle in the coastal city of Jaffa; the Jews moved a few miles up the beach and began to build the city that is now home to over one million people. That same year also saw the birth of the first kibbutz, Kibbutz Degania on the Sea of Galilee.

As more and more Jews came to settle on the newly bought land in Israel, a need developed to speak a common language. People from all over the world were uniting with a common goal, but not with a common language. Eliezer Ben Yehudah and his family took it upon themselves to revive the Hebrew language, which had been lying dormant for years. (Jews used it for prayer and study but not for daily speech.) Ben Yehudah taught his family to speak Hebrew and then proceeded to teach others. He wrote the first modern Hebrew dictionary, assigning new meanings to ancient words and creating new words for things such as television, newspaper, and airplane. The language was revived in one generation, a remarkable feat considering that Hebrew is the only "dead" language ever to be successfully revived.

When World War I broke out, Jews fought on both sides, some with the Turks who ruled in "Palestine" and some on the side of the British. At the end of the war, England gained control of Palestine (the name given to the area by the Romans; it means Philistines).

In the Balfour Declaration of 1917, the British pledged their support for a Jewish homeland in Palestine, even though over the years they had also made similar promises to the Arabs of the area. When there were anti-Jewish riots in Israel, the English did little to stop them. Throughout the 1930s Jews attempted to immigrate to Israel in order to escape persecution in Europe. The British, caving in to Arab pressure, restricted immigration to that area, and boatloads of Jews were imprisoned on the island of Cyprus rather than being allowed to enter Israel.

Finally, in 1947 the United Nations voted to partition Palestine into both a Jewish and an Arab state. The Jews accepted this plan, but the Arabs did not, so as Israel announced its Declaration of Independence, it was invaded by the armies of the neighboring Arab states.

Despite the odds, Israel survived the attacks and remains to this day a state struggling for its survival in a sea of enemies. A rich Jewish culture has grown up there, both religious and secular, a testament to Jewish strength and tenacity.

Introducing the Lesson

You might want to begin this lesson by discussing birthdays. Ask the children to tell when their birthdays are, and to describe how they celebrate.

Explain to your students that everything has a birthday, whether it be a person, an animal, a plant, or even a country. On the board, list some famous birthdays, such as George Washington, Martin Luther King, yourself, the world (Rosh Hashanah), trees (Tu B'Shevat), America (July 4), and Israel (the fifth of Iyar). Discuss how each of these birthdays is celebrated.

Then ask each child how old he or she is. Ask how they know. Ask them if they know how old Israel is. Help the class figure it out, and then help them to imagine a cake with that many candles on it.

Finally, show pictures of famous places in the Land of Israel. Explain that as we learn about Israel's birthday, we are also going to learn a bit about the people and places of that special land.

Teaching the Text

Israel's Birthday Explain that Israel declared its independence somewhat like the United States did—by drafting a Declaration of Independence.

Never Forgetting Israel Ask the children if they know where their families came from. Point out that Jews have lived all over the world during the last two thousand years. Ask if anyone knows Jews that speak languages other than English because they lived in different countries.

Jewish people were scattered across the world . . . Use a large map to point out the locations of some of the countries in which Jews have lived. Talk about the routes people might have taken to get to those places from Israel and why they might have needed to go there.

We spoke of our love for Israel in our prayers . . . Point out how the arks in most synagogues face east toward Jerusalem.

Returning to the Land Discuss the reasons why Jews needed a land of their own. (They were not always welcome in other countries. Sometimes they were thrown out or persecuted for being Jewish.)

They drained the muddy swamps . . . The Jews took a desert land that could not grow any food and learned how to make it productive. How did Israelis learn to grow food in the desert? Why did they need to plant so many new trees? What did they need to build? (They used water running through pipes that have little holes in them to let only a drip of water out at a time. They planted trees for soil conservation, shade, and beauty. They built entire communities—houses, roads, school, stores, sewers, water pipes—where there had been none.)

Independence When Israel was attacked by its neighbors, how was the Jewish victory like the victory of the Maccabees in the Hanukkah story?

Returning to Israel Ask your students to name some of the reasons Jews came to live in Israel. Do they still come today? (They came to escape persecution in other countries or to find new homes after theirs were destroyed in the Holocaust. They also came out of a conviction that it was important for Jews to live in Israel and build a strong Jewish state. Jews are still coming even today, especially from the countries of Russia and Ethiopia.)

An Ancient Language Comes to Life Eliezer Ben Yehudah taught his family to speak Hebrew. His son was not allowed to speak any other language and was the only Hebrew-speaking child of his day. (He must have been a little lonely.) But by the time he was an adult, many Jews in Israel could speak Hebrew. Tell your class the story of the tower of Babel and discuss how reviving Hebrew was the opposite of that story. Jews who spoke many different languages could now work together because they were able to speak one common language—Hebrew.

There is a legend . . . This is a very famous midrash that explains why the site of the Temple was on Mount Moriah (also known as Mount Zion). After reading the story of the two brothers, you might have the class discuss the following questions:

      1. How did the two brothers feel about each other? Is that the way you feel about your siblings?

      2. How did they show their feelings? How do you show yours?

      3. Did God like the way the brothers acted? How does God want us to act toward our brothers and sisters?

      4. The actions of the brothers made a place holy. Can our actions make places special too?

Perhaps the class would like to illustrate the story.

Celebration How is the celebration of Israel's birthday like a person's birthday party? (We dance and sing and have good things to eat. We honor the one whose birthday it is. We sing "Hatikvah" instead of "Happy Birthday.")

Suggested Activities

1. **Make an Israeli flag.** Instructions can be found on page 205 of *Integrating Arts and Crafts in the Jewish School*. Be sure to discuss the symbol of the star (the Magen David was the symbol on the shield of King David).

2. **Show pictures of famous places in Israel.** Discuss what it is like to be there. Perhaps you can invite someone to class who has been to Israel to share some of his or her pictures and experiences.

3. **Make a simple map of Israel.** Have the class color the water blue, draw a wall around Jerusalem, color the desert brown, make tall buildings in Tel Aviv, on so on.

4. **Cook an Israeli dish.** Hummus and falafel are popular.

5. **Eat the foods of Israel.** Figs, dates, olives, oranges, and other foods can be enjoyed by the group. Say the proper blessings before you eat.

6. **Make a mural of the cities of Israel.** See pages 198-200 of *Integrating Arts and Crafts in the Jewish School.*

7. **Teach your students to dance a hora or some other Israeli dance.**

8. **Perform an Israeli tzedakah project such as planting trees in Israel through the Jewish National Fund.**

9. **Learn some popular Hebrew phrases, such as *Shalom* and *L'hitraot.*** You might want to teach the Hebrew names of some common foods and ask your students to pretend that they are in an Israeli restaurant and must order the foods in Hebrew.

10. **Teach the following songs:**

"Im Tirtzu" (This is the text of Theodor Herzl's statement, "If you will it, it is no dream.)

"Hatikvah"
"Hine Ma Tov"
"Shalom Haverim"
"Am Yisrael Hai"
"Lo Yisa Goi El Goi Herev"

FAMILY EDUCATION IDEAS ARE LOCATED AT THE END OF THIS GUIDE

SHAVUOT

(Text pages 148-159)

Important concepts

1. On Shavuot we celebrate the giving of the Torah. We remember the time when Moses went up Mount Sinai to receive the Torah from God.
2. On Shavuot we read the Ten Commandments in synagogue.
3. We count the seven weeks between Passover and Shavuot. This period of time is known as the Omer.
4. Shavuot also celebrates the early wheat harvest in Israel.
5. Shavuot is known as one of the three pilgrimage festivals. In ancient days, farmers brought the first fruits of their fields to the Temple in Jerusalem and offered them to God.
6. It is customary to eat foods made of milk or milk products on Shavuot.

Vocabulary

Counting the Omer We count the seven weeks between Passover and Shavuot. This period of time is known as the Omer. It was the time that lapsed between the planting of the wheat and its harvest. It is traditional to recite a short prayer each day of the Omer to count off the days. It is also customary not to have weddings during this period of time except on one intervening holiday, Lag B'omer.

Mount Sinai This is the traditional site where we believe Moses climbed to receive the Torah from God. According to the description in the Torah, the top of the mountain was covered with clouds and smoke. Thunder and lightning flashed, and Moses remained there for forty days and forty nights.

Shavuot The Hebrew word for "weeks." This holiday earned the name Shavuot because of the seven weeks we count between Passover and Shavuot's arrival. Shavuot is also known as "the Harvest Festival" and "the Festival of First Fruits."

Ten Commandments Ten of the laws that Moses received on Mount Sinai. They are repeated twice in the Torah in their entirety and are held up as a model of proper ethical behavior.

Background Information

How Shavuot Began

The winter snows have melted; the first buds of spring have blossomed and begun to bear fruit. Passover, with its exacting preparations and animated celebrations, now fades into the past. Our attention turns to final exams and closing exercises that are a part of the end of the school year.

At this time in late spring comes Shavuot, a holiday much less noticed than Passover, a holiday sometimes almost forgotten on our Jewish schedule of events. I have often wondered why this is so—whether it is our lack of interest in the Israeli wheat harvest or the fact that we are still worn out from Passover. Shavuot needs a second look. By playing down this celebration, we are losing the opportunity to celebrate Torah and the revelation at Sinai, which in Jewish history stands as the pivotal event of our past.

Ever since the destruction of the Temple in 70 C.E., the Jewish people have not truly been tied to the land for their sustenance. Even before that date fewer and fewer Jews were making their living as farmers. The importance of the agricultural festival of Shavuot, which marked the end of the barley harvest and the beginning of the early wheat harvest, decreased. The Sadducees, who stressed the importance of sacrifices and offerings at the Temple, made much of this pilgrimage festival. Jews from all over would bring their first fruits to Jerusalem and offer them to God. But the Sadducees were losing power, and the Pharisees were gaining control.

The Pharisees saw the Torah, the law itself, as the place where God and Jews met. They therefore sought to elevate the importance of Torah in every way. At that time there was no specific anniversary celebration for of the giving of the Torah. The Torah itself mentions no special day. The Pharisees took advantage of this faltering agricultural holiday and imbued it with new meaning. They changed the focus of the holiday and began to call it Shavuot, "the season of the giving of the Torah."

Today we count seven weeks between Passover and Shavuot, the exact amount of time it takes for wheat to grow and mature. Since we don't all grow wheat, we can instead imagine that we have just left Egypt and are wandering in the desert, all the while making our way toward Mount Sinai. After seven weeks we arrive at the foot of the mountain. We feel the thunder and the lightning, stand back as the mountain smokes before us, and witness Moses as he comes down, all aglow with the tablets in his hands.

There is a Hasidic notion that all Jewish souls were at Sinai, that the young and old of every age and time witnessed this revelation. (Once at a party I mentioned to a certain man that he looked familiar but that I just couldn't place his face. He smiled and said that we had probably met at Sinai.) And it is in this wonderful, comforting notion that we receive our strength. One day we touched God through the gift of Torah, and we remember that day once a year. This remembrance renews our strength and helps us to touch God over and over again.

The holiday of Shavuot is mentioned several times in the Torah. It is called the feast of "Weeks," a name derived from the counting of the seven weeks between Passover and Shavuot. It is also called *Hag Hakatsir*, "Harvest Festival," and *Hag Habikkurim*, or "Festival of the First Fruits."

Since Shavuot is one of the pilgrimage festivals, long ago the Jews brought their first fruits to Jerusalem as an offering to God. The wheat was brought in the form of baked bread, symbolizing man's partnership with God. God gives the wheat, but it is the labor of man that turns it into bread. Today it is customary to decorate one's home and synagogue with flowers and green plants to recall the harvest aspect of the holiday.

Celebrating Shavuot

On Shavuot evening we light holiday candles with the "Yom tov" blessing and say the holiday Kiddush over wine. It is traditional to serve a dairy meal, for the Torah tells us that the Land of Israel was flowing with "milk and honey." Some people like to follow the Hasidic custom of staying up all night to study Torah to heighten the experience of the revelation the next day.

The service in the synagogue includes the reciting of Hallel, Psalms 113-118, and the reciting of a special poem called "Akdamot." This piece was written by Rabbi Meir ben Isaac Nehorai of Germany in the twelfth century. It is a joyous song that celebrates our commitment to Torah.

The Torah reading on the first day of Shavuot is Exodus 19 and 20. It contains a description of the giving of the Torah and a recitation of the Ten Commandments. This is one of the most dramatic Torah portions of the entire year, offering many opportunities for imaginative visualizations of the event. The haftarah is a description of the vision of

Ezekiel. Both these pieces stress that any individual can hear God's voice and that the revelation was for everyone.

Conservative, Reconstructionist, and Orthodox Jews of the Diaspora celebrate two days of Shavuot, although only one day is celebrated among Reform Jews and in Israel. The second day is traditionally known as both the birthday and the day of the death of King David. It is a day that we set aside to recite Yizkor.

Shavuot is also a time when we read Megillat Ruth. This wonderful book is about the woman we consider to be the first *Ger*, or Jew by choice. Years later Ruth became the grandmother of King David himself.

In the past it was traditional to begin a child's Jewish education on Shavuot. Children were brought to the school and given honey to lick off their slates, a symbolic act showing them that the words of Torah are sweet. Today it has become customary to hold Confirmation ceremonies on this day. This relatively recent ceremony, supported by Reform and some Conservative synagogues, gives young people the opportunity to affirm publicly their commitment to Torah.

Introducing the Lesson

Bring the class into the sanctuary to see the Torah. Let them examine the ark, the Torah covers, and the silver crowns, and ask them what all these special items tell us about our attitude toward Torah. (We keep the Torah in a special cabinet that is very ornate and decorated with artwork. It is very safe inside. We cover the Torah with fancy embroidered velvet, like a person's best party dress or most handsome clothes. We dress the Torah in beautiful and expensive silver. The Torah itself is made by hand, not by machine, and takes a long time to complete. It is a labor of love for a scribe to make a Torah. Each Torah is exactly alike because we want to be sure that nothing in it is changed.)

Discuss these points with the class as you examine the Torah. Explain that we feel the Torah is extra special because it was given to us as a gift from God. In it are the things that God wants to tell us and the things that God asks us to do.

Explain to the class that there was a very special day when God gave us the Torah. It was very exciting and very mysterious. The holiday of Shavuot celebrates that day, and we are about to learn more about it.

Teaching the Stories

The Ten Commandments (text pages 151-152) The Torah describes the scene at the foot of Mount Sinai with a fair amount of detail (Exodus 19). The people camped at the foot of the mountain. They were told to prepare for the revelation for three days. On the third day the mountain was covered in smoke. There were thunder and lightning and the sound of the horn. The people trembled and stood far off. Moses went up the mountain, and God descended in a cloud. "Moses spoke, and God answered him by a voice" (Exodus 19:19).

The story on page 152 of the textbook serves to embellish the Torah account, as all midrashim do. There is much potential for creating your own midrash around this scene. It is full of human drama and emotion, as it is the account of the moment when the Jewish people came in the closest contact with God.

Read or describe Exodus 19 to the class. Have the group add their own details to the scene to create their own midrashim. Perhaps there was a deaf child who could not hear God's voice. Perhaps one person tried to break through the barrier established by Moses, or maybe the sound of the horn turned into swirling smoke. Use your imagination and have fun with it.

There is a legend that when Moses was on Mount Sinai . . . (text pages 153-154) This story is a popular midrash that evolved from the revelation in Exodus 19. Have the class read the story, and ask the following questions to spark discussion:

1. Why did God want something in return for the Torah?
2. What items did the people offer? Why did they think that these were good gifts?
3. Why did God not accept the jewelry, rubies, and emeralds?
4. Did God accept the gift of "teaching the children"? What does this tell us about how God feels about children?
5. What does this story teach us about the value of learning?
6. What does this story teach us about the value of learning Torah?

Teaching the Text

The Gift of Torah It is important to stress the *we* in describing these events. *We* left Egypt. *We* wandered in the desert, and *we* stood at the foot of Mount Sinai to receive the Torah. These exciting events are a part of every Jew's experience.

Let the children imagine themselves at the foot of Mount Sinai as Moses went up to receive the Torah. Read or tell the details from Exodus 19. Ask the children how they would feel and what they would be thinking. Ask them why Moses got to go up the mountain when everyone else had to stay below. (The last line of the Torah tells us that Moses was the only person who ever saw God face to face.)

You might also add that the period of seven weeks that we count from Passover to Shavuot is called the Omer.

The Ten Commandments See how many of the Ten Commandments the children can name. Have them practice saying them as a group until the class can name them all. Point out that some of the commandments are things we should do and some are things we shouldn't do. Ask the children why they think we stand in synagogue while the Ten Commandments are being read.

In some synagogues people stay up late at night . . . Ask the children what it must feel like to stay up late to study. Also explain what Confirmation is. Discuss why that might be a part of the Shavuot celebration. (The day that we celebrate the giving of the Torah is a good time to affirm our commitment to Torah publicly.)

We all look forward to special times . . .(picture caption) We cross off the days on the calendar as we do when we are waiting for any special day to come. Ask the children if they count the days before other special days (birthdays, vacations, etc.).

Counting the Omer *Omer* is the Hebrew word for "sheaf." Seven weeks is the exact time it takes to grow wheat. Try to show a picture of a wheat field. Discuss with the class how that soft flowing plant turns into bread. Bread was the item that was brought to the Temple and offered to God. This offering shows that people work in partnership with God, for it takes God to make the wheat but it takes people to make the bread.

You might also want to show what barley looks like. This was a very important food in Temple days, and most children today don't know what it looks like.

From all over the Land of Israel . . . Describe what took place on the pilgrimage festivals. Review the other two pilgrimage festivals, Sukkot and Passover. (There were no local synagogues, so all the people traveled to one Temple three times each year.) The children might want to act out the scene.

A Land of Milk and Honey Have the children name foods made from dairy products.

Suggested Activities

1. Play a game to memorize the Ten Commandments.

Sit in a circle. The first child says the first commandment. The second child says the first and second commandment, and so on until all ten have been added.

Play telephone with one of the Ten Commandments. See if the one at the end of the chain is the same as the one that began the chain.

3. Learn to draw the Ten Commandments in the form of two tablets. The children need to write the numbers one to ten with Hebrew letters. (Alef, bet, gimmel, etc.)

4. Prepare blintzes.

5. Make an Omer chart and mark off the days in class together.

FAMILY EDUCATION IDEAS ARE LOCATED AT THE END OF THIS GUIDE

FAMILY EDUCATION EXPERIENCES

Activities   Projects   Events

On the following pages you will find a variety of materials to use with the families of your students.

Feel free to select the activities and events you deem most useful in your school setting and to duplicate and send home the Parent/Child worksheets you find appropriate.

It is most effective to implement Family Education holiday experiences a week or two before the actual celebration takes place.

HIGH HOLY DAYS

Rosh Hashanah

1. Bake a round ḥallah or make taigelach and other desserts that use honey. This project can be done by the entire class and invited parents.

2. Have families learn how to do Tashlich together. Plan to perform this ritual as a group after services on the holiday.

3. Plan a family service at the synagogue on Rosh Hashanah. Invite the children to attend with their parents.

Yom Kippur

1. Encourage families to attend the children's service on Yom Kippur. If your synagogue doesn't have one, encourage your rabbi to start one.

2. Encourage parents to bring children to the Ne'ilah service at the end of the day to hear the final blast of the shofar.

ROSH HASHANA GREETINGS

Sending New Year cards is a nice way of keeping in touch with friends and of strengthening family ties. Make it a family experience. Decide on your list of recipients. Choose appropriate cards, and make each card special with personal messages. Even addressing, stuffing, and stamping the envelopes can be fun for the family to do together!

Would you like your Rosh Hashanah cards to be not only *from* the members of your family, but *by* them as well? Here is one way of printing your own family greeting cards.

YOU WILL NEED:

- *Styrofoam (about ⅛" thick)*
- *Cardboard (from a cardboard carton)*
- *Blank cards (you can cut them from drawing paper)*
- *Envelopes*

- *Glue*
- *Poster or acrylic paints*
- *Brushes*
- *Scissors*

HERE'S HOW TO DO IT:

1. Cut the styrofoam pieces into various designs. (If your designs include lettering, it must be done backwards, since printing produces a reverse image.)

Glue the designs onto the piece of cardboard. Do not overlap them. Let dry. This is your "printing plate."

2. Brush paint over the printing plate.

3. While the paint is still wet, turn the printing plate over and press the wet surface onto a blank greeting card. Press lightly. Lift the plate gently from the card. Repeat the process to print as many cards as you need. Let the cards dry.

WE SENT SPECIAL NEW YEAR GREETINGS TO:

_____   _____

_____   _____

_____   _____

_____   _____

_____   _____

Family Education Experience (Rosh Hashanah), *My Jewish Year*, Behrman House, Inc.

SUKKOT

1. Offer a sukkah-building workshop for parents who might be considering building a sukkah for the first time.

2. Have a family day at your synagogue on which families can help build and decorate the synagogue sukkah. Encourage families to return for a morning service, when the children can have the opportunity to wave the lulav in the sukkah.

3. Encourage families that build sukkot to organize a sukkah-hopping party. After agreeing on a day, publish a schedule of the time each family will have an open sukkah for guests. The community can then move from one sukkah to another.

Building a Sukkah

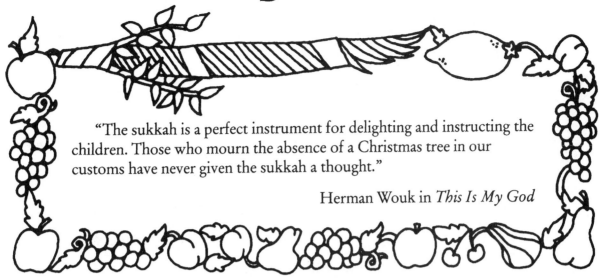

"The sukkah is a perfect instrument for delighting and instructing the children. Those who mourn the absence of a Christmas tree in our customs have never given the sukkah a thought."

Herman Wouk in *This Is My God*

Why not build a family sukkah? It's not hard to do. You can build it right in your own backyard. Or if you live in an apartment, check out the possibilities of erecting a sukkah on the roof (perhaps together with other Jewish families in your building).

HOW TO BUILD A SUKKAH

According to tradition:

- *Start building the sukkah right after Yom Kippur.*
- *If there is not enough material to make 4 walls, erect 3 complete walls, rather than 4 incomplete ones.*
- *The sukkah can be built in a variety of ways, but its roof is special. It is made of leafy branches in sufficient quantity so that there is more shade than sun inside the sukkah, but there is still enough space to see the stars at night.*

You can build your sukkah with a wide assortment of materials. 2 x 4 standards and canvas are often used for the walls. But don't hesitate to improvise with available materials. The important thing is for you and your children to build together.

Be sure to decorate your sukkah with a colorful assortment of fall leaves, flowers, fruits, and vegetables. Hang them from the roof with string. Also your children can display their artwork on the walls. It is a mitzvah to make the sukkah as beautiful as possible.

Then enjoy your family sukkah to its fullest. Eat dinner in it. Sing and talk in it. Sleep in it if you can. Unroll those sleeping bags.

Happy Sukkot!

SIMḤAT TORAH

1. Assign themes to the seven hakkafot (concepts such as mercy, lovingkindness, justice, etc.). Ask a family or group of families to prepare a banner, a dance, or a song for each theme and to lead the congregation in their theme during one of the hakkafot on Simḥat Torah.

2. Have the children in the religious school make banners that represent the different parshiot (portions) of the Torah. They can carry them on Simḥat Torah.

3. Write different sections from the Torah on slips of paper and distribute them to the families present for the Simḥat Torah celebration. See if they can line themselves up in order as the pieces occur in the Torah.

4. Send home a brief explanation of the holiday Simḥat Torah with instructions on how to make a flag for the event, and a recipe for jelly apples.

Simḥat Torah Family Craft

On Simḥat Torah, there are no spectators; everyone participates. Even pre-Bar and Bat Mitzvah youngsters play an active role in the services. They are invited to say a blessing over the Torah together. A large prayer shawl, a tallit, is held over their heads as they recite the prayers in unison.

As the Torah scrolls are carried around the synagogue, everyone joins in and follows along. There are seven hakkafot in all. A family banner to carry during the Torah processions can heighten your sense of participation in the celebration.

SIMḤAT TORAH FAMILY BANNER

YOU WILL NEED:

- *Roll of white wrapping paper or an old sheet*
- *Felt markers*
- *2 wooden dowels*
- *Masking tape*
- *Stapler*
- *And lots of imagination*

HERE'S HOW TO DO IT:

There are really no rules. Each member of the family can sign the banner and write a family holiday wish. You can attach family photographs, drawings, and greeting cards. Let the banner show what is special about your family. Let the banner reflect your family's special interests. When you are finished, staple or tape the banner onto the wooden dowels and then be sure to come to synagogue and *celebrate!*

Family Education Experience (Simḥat Torah), *My Jewish Year*, Behrman House, Inc.

SHABBAT

1. Encourage your students to attend a family or children's service if your synagogue offers one. If not, encourage your rabbi to begin this sort of activity.

2. Suggest to your students that they attend Shabbat dinners at the synagogue. These are usually fun, family experiences, where many families can light candles together and enjoy dinner in the synagogue setting. The dinner can begin or be followed by an abbreviated children's service.

3. Encourage family participation in a "Shabbat Workshop" in which activities are provided for families to learn ways in which they can keep Shabbat. Activities might include baking ḥallah, learning blessings, making Kiddush cups and ḥallah covers, or having discussions of Talmudic texts on the subject.

4. Teach parents how to bless their children.

Lighting Sabbath Candles

The Sabbath is ushered into the Jewish home when the Shabbat candles are lit and blessed. According to custom, at least two candles must be lit, for Shabbat is a time of brightness and beauty. The ceremony takes place just prior to sunset *on Friday evening.

- *Light the candles (the Sabbath candles are lit* **before** *the blessing is recited, because it is forbidden to kindle a flame once Shabbat has begun).*

- *Move your hands around the flames, and bring them toward your face. This gesture symbolically welcomes the Sabbath into your home.*

- *Place your hands over your eyes, so that you will not see the Sabbath lights until you have recited the blessing. The prayer blesses God for giving us this mitzvah to perform:*

בָּרוּךְ אַתָּה יְיָ אֱלֹהֵינוּ מֶלֶךְ הָעוֹלָם אֲשֶׁר קִדְּשָׁנוּ בְּמִצְוֹתָיו וְצִוָּנוּ לְהַדְלִיק נֵר שֶׁל שַׁבָּת.

Baruch atah adonai elohenu melech ha-olam asher kidshanu b'mitzvotav v'tzivanu l'hadlik ner shel Shabbat.

Blessed are You, Adonai our God, Ruler of the world, who makes us holy with mitzvot and commands us to kindle the Sabbath lights.

- *Take another moment to recite a personal prayer for those you love.*

- *Remove your hands from your face and open your eyes. You have completed the mitzvah. Shabbat has arrived in your home. Shabbat Shalom!*

CANDLE LIGHTING TIMES

Hebrew Date	English Date	Time	✔

* Sabbath candles may be lit, at the earliest, 1¼ hours before sunset, but the usual time is 18 minutes before sunset.

BLESSINGS OVER WINE AND HALLAH

Your family gathers at the table to begin the special Friday evening Sabbath meal. Everything—tablecloth, dishes, silverware, flowers—should be arranged with care. Make the sabbath meal as beautiful as possible. The ḥallah is covered with a cloth and the Kiddush cup is filled with wine. Bread and wine are special foods in Jewish tradition, for they symbolize a blending of God's generosity and human achievement. God has given the grape and the grain; we have made them into wine and bread.

BLESSING THE WINE

Everyone joins in the recitation of the blessing over the wine:

בָּרוּךְ אַתָּה יְיָ אֱלֹהֵינוּ מֶלֶךְ הָעוֹלָם בּוֹרֵא פְּרִי הַגָּפֶן.

Baruch atah adonai elohenu melech ha-olam boray p'ri hagafen.

Blessed are You, Adonai our God, Ruler of the world, creator of the fruit of the vine.

BLESSING THE ḤALLAH

Two loaves of ḥallah dramatize the idea that Shabbat is a special day. During our everyday meals we serve only one loaf of bread; on the Sabbath and holy days we celebrate with two. While wandering in the desert, the Children of Israel received a daily portion of manna from God. On Friday of each week, however, God sent down a double portion so that they would not have to work gathering food on the Sabbath. Thus the two Sabbath loaves. (If you make your own ḥallah, Shabbat will be even more special.)

Everyone joins in the recitation of the blessing over bread:

בָּרוּךְ אַתָּה יְיָ אֱלֹהֵינוּ מֶלֶךְ הָעוֹלָם הַמּוֹצִיא לֶחֶם מִן הָאָרֶץ.

Baruch atah adonai elohenu melech ha-olam ha-motzi leḥem min ha-aretz.

Blessed are You, Adonai our God, Ruler of the world, who brings forth bread from the earth.

Blessing Your Children

Before the recitation of the Kiddush, it is traditional to bless your children. Here is how to do it. Place your hands on your child's head and recite the following blessing:

For sons:

יְשִׂימְךָ אֱלֹהִים כְּאֶפְרַיִם וְכִמְנַשֶּׁה:

Y'si-m'cha elohim k'efraim v'chi-menasheh.

May God make you as Ephraim and Menasseh.

For daughters:

יְשִׂימֵךְ אֱלֹהִים כְּשָׂרָה רִבְקָה רָחֵל וְלֵאָה:

Y'si-mech elohim k'Sara Rivka Raḥel v'Leah.

May God make you as Sarah, Rebecca, Rachel, and Leah.

Then add, for all the children:

יְבָרֶכְךָ יְיָ וְיִשְׁמְרֶךָ:
יָאֵר יְיָ פָּנָיו אֵלֶיךָ וִיחֻנֶּךָּ:
יִשָּׂא יְיָ פָּנָיו אֵלֶיךָ. וְיָשֵׂם לְךָ שָׁלוֹם:

Y'varech'cha adonai v'yishm'recha.
Ya'er adonai panav aylecha viḥuneka.
Yisa adonai panav aylecha v'yasem l'cha shalom.

May God bless and keep you.
May God's light shine on you and be good to you.
May God's light shine on you and give you peace.

You may add your own words as well. Make this moment of religious communication between you and your child personal and special.

Family Education Experience (Shabbat), *My Jewish Year*, Behrman House, Inc.

ḤANUKKAH

1. Sponsor a menorah-making contest in your synagogue. Give the children the assignment of making a menorah with their family at home. After they are done, they should present the menorah to the class. You can even offer prizes in different categories. Offer suggestions and show samples to give ideas. You might send home a flyer describing the contest and offering suggestions. You will be surprised how many creative entries you receive.

2. Have your synagogue sponsor a Ḥanukkah party. You can serve Ḥanukkah foods such as latkes and can make ice cream sundaes (using candies to make the face of Judah Maccabee on the scoops of ice cream). The party can have entertainment, such as a menorah-making contest, a joke-telling contest, a talent show, a small play.

Lighting the Ḥanukkah Candles

Did you know that in ancient times there was a difference of opinion as to how to celebrate Ḥanukkah? The students of one rabbi, Shammai, believed that the celebration of Ḥanukkah should begin with eight candles, taking one away each night. The students of Hillel insisted upon starting with one candle and then adding one more each night. The school of Rabbi Hillel prevailed because "holiness is something that must grow, not diminish." And the spirit of holiness needs to be communicated and shared. Therefore it is a mitzvah to place the Ḥanukkah lights at a window facing the street.

LIGHTING THE ḤANUKKAH MENORAH

As you face the Ḥanukkah menorah, place the first candle on your right; subsequent candles are added to the left.

Light the shamash, then take it in your hand and say:

בָּרוּךְ אַתָּה יְיָ אֱלֹהֵינוּ מֶלֶךְ הָעוֹלָם אֲשֶׁר קִדְּשָׁנוּ בְּמִצְוֹתָיו וְצִוָּנוּ לְהַדְלִיק נֵר שֶׁל חֲנֻכָּה.

Baruch atah adonai elohenu melech ha-olam asher kidshanu b'mitzvotav v'tzivanu l'hadlik ner shel Ḥanukkah.

Blessed are You, Adonai our God, Ruler of the world, who makes us holy with mitzvot and commands us to kindle the Ḥanukkah lights.

בָּרוּךְ אַתָּה יְיָ אֱלֹהֵינוּ מֶלֶךְ הָעוֹלָם שֶׁעָשָׂה נִסִּים לַאֲבוֹתֵינוּ בַּיָּמִים הָהֵם בַּזְּמַן הַזֶּה.

Baruch atah adonai elohenu melech ha-olam she'asah nisim la-avotaynu ba-yamim ha-hem bazman hazeh.

Blessed are You, Adonai our God, Ruler of the world, who did wondrous things for our people long ago at this time of year.

Now light the candles. The new candle is always kindled first.
On the first night of Ḥanukkah, a third blessing is also recited:

בָּרוּךְ אַתָּה יְיָ אֱלֹהֵינוּ מֶלֶךְ הָעוֹלָם שֶׁהֶחֱיָנוּ וְקִיְּמָנוּ וְהִגִּיעָנוּ לַזְּמַן הַזֶּה.

Baruch atah adonai elohenu melech ha-olam sheheḥeyanu v'kiye-manu v'hi-gi-anu lazman hazeh.

Blessed are You, Adonai our God, Ruler of the world, who has given us life, sustained us, and brought us to this season of joy.

Family Education Experience (Ḥanukkah), *My Jewish Year*, Behrman House, Inc.

Ḥanukkah Recipe

What would Ḥanukkah be like without potato pancakes?

We eat latkes fried in oil to remember the miracle of the cruse of oil at the Maccabean rededication of the Temple.

LATKES

- *4 large or 6 medium potatoes*
- *1 medium-sized onion*
- *1 teaspoon salt*
- *1 egg, well beaten*
- *3 tablespoons matzah meal*
- *½ teaspoon baking powder*
- *vegetable oil for frying*

1. Grate raw potatoes that have been washed and pared.

2. Grate the onion and add it to the potatoes.

3. Add salt, egg, and matzah meal mixed with the baking powder. Beat all ingredients well into a smooth, thin batter. If the batter seems too watery, add a little more matzah meal.

4. Drop the batter by tablespoonfuls into hot oil in a heavy frying pan. The oil must be deep enough to almost cover the latke. Brown on one side and, with a pancake turner, turn the latke to brown on the other side. Drain on absorbent paper. Serve piping hot. Delicious when served with applesauce or sour cream.

   Serves 4.

   Note: Do not fry more than three or four latkes at the same time. Too many cooked at once will cool the oil and keep the latkes from being crisp and tender.

Family Education Experience (Ḥanukkah), *My Jewish Year*, Behrman House, Inc.

Ḥanukkah Family Readings

The First Commandment: "Thou shalt have no other gods before Me. Thou shalt not make unto thee a graven image."

The Maccabean uprising (which we celebrate on Ḥanukkah) took place because our ancestors refused to abandon God. They refused to worship idols. Judaism's pivotal contribution to religious thought has been monotheism, and our greatest spiritual danger, idolatry. We hope that you will read these two selections to your children.

ABRAM SEEKS GOD

One night Abram gazed up at the stars and marveled, "How beautiful are the moon and stars! They must be gods." He bowed before them and worshipped.

The night passed, and the sun rose. "The warmth and light of the sun," Abram observed, "have driven away the moon and the stars. Surely the sun is god over all!" He bowed before the sun and worshipped.

But clouds came and hid the light of the sun. Then a wind drove the clouds before it. Abram realized that all these were but part of the world and its wonders. "There must be a ruler over all the world," he thought, "over the sun, the moon, and the stars and over all the creatures of the earth. I shall worship only the Creator and Ruler of the universe."

And Abram bowed before the unseen God and spoke a prayer in his heart.

THE IDOL SMASHER

Abram (Abraham's original name, before it was changed by God) looked at the rows of idols around him and picked up an axe. He smashed all but the largest of them and put the axe in its hands. When Teraḥ, his father, returned, he found his shop littered with pottery fragments. Only the large idol remained whole. "Who has done this?" he cried.

Abram was ready with an answer. "The idols were hungry. I brought them food. But the big god seized the axe, killed the others, and ate all the food himself."

Teraḥ stared at his son. "Abram, you are mocking me! You know that idols can neither move nor eat!"

Then Abram said, "Father, let your ears hear what your tongue speaks."

THINGS TO TALK ABOUT

Why do you think that ancient peoples worshipped objects of wood or stone? What was the idols' great attraction? What needs did they fulfill?

If you were Abram, how would you explain the various ideas that led to the discovery of One God? Do people worship idols today? (Idolatry has not disappeared; it has merely "gone modern." The idols of today include money, status, success, possessions, youth, beauty, etc. These are not in themselves evil; rather it is a question of attitudes and values.)

Family Education Experience (Ḥanukkah), *My Jewish Year*, Behrman House, Inc.

PURIM

1. Have your families prepare mishloaḥ manot baskets to share with friends or to offer to the poor. Each family can also be assigned a nursing home resident to bring their basket to. Doing this gives families the opportunity not only to give the basket, but to make a visit as well. The baskets can contain any kind of fruit and treats. Hamantashen are traditional. Children can share their baskets with other students at the synagogue Purim celebration.

2. Offer parents suggestions on how to prepare a costume for Purim. Send home a simple version of the Purim story so that the child can choose a character. Stress that adults as well as children can dress up. Offer prizes for the best-dressed adults as well as the best-dressed children.

3. Encourage families to attend the Purim festivities at your synagogue. Children should attend the Megillah reading with their parents. Perhaps they can bring a homemade gragger that they made with their parents.

Purim Recipe

On Purim we eat hamantashen, a three-cornered cookie filled with fruit or poppy seeds. The literal translation of *hamantashen* is "Haman's pockets," but over the years it has come to symbolize Haman's three-cornered hat and, indeed, the headgear of any tyrant who would try to destroy us.

This recipe is guaranteed to enhance the atmosphere of good feeling that is such an important part of the Purim celebration. Try it. You and your children will enjoy the results.

HAMANTASHEN

For the dough:

- *½ cup butter*
- *1 cup sugar*
- *1 egg*
- *1 tablespoon milk*
- *1 tablespoon vanilla extract*
- *2 cups sifted flour*
- *2 teaspoons baking powder*
- *¼ teaspoon salt*

For the filling:

- *your favorite jam or jelly*

1. Soften the butter by rubbing it with the back of a wooden spoon. This is called "creaming."

2. Add the sugar gradually and beat the mixture until it's fluffy.

3. Add the egg, milk, and vanilla and beat well.

4. Sift together the flour, salt, and baking powder.

5. Stir the sifted ingredients into the mixture to make a soft dough. Chill the dough in the refrigerator for 20 minutes.

6. Sprinkle a board lightly with flour. Roll the dough out on the board until it is about ⅛ inch thick. Using a round cutter dipped in flour, cut into circles about 3 inches in diameter.

7. Place a heaping teaspoonful of jam on each circle. Bring three sides of the circle together to form a triangle. Pinch the edges together to make a seam.

8. Arrange the hamantashen far apart on an ungreased cookie sheet. Bake in a hot oven (400°F) for 10 to 12 minutes.

Makes about 36 hamantashen.

Family Education Experience (Purim), *My Jewish Year*, Behrman House, Inc.

PASSOVER

1. Plan to have a Model Seder as a part of your religious school schedule. Children can recite sections from the Haggadah and eat the symbolic foods of the holiday. Parents can also participate in this event.

2. Have a Passover Fair. Create booths on different topics that pertain to the holiday and have families circulate from one booth to another. You can even have tickets and prizes. Some possible booths might be: recite the blessings and win a prize, make matzah, make ḥaroset, go through a cross-the-sea obstacle course.

Passover Symbols

Can you and your children identify these Passover objects? Do you know what they symbolize?

You can use this sheet as your partial Passover "shopping list."
You will need all of these for your seder.

Answers:
1. Matzah 2. Zeroa (shank bone) 3. Maror (bitter herb) 4. Haroset (apples, nuts, and wine)
5. Karpas (parsley or lettuce) 6. Salt Water 7. Betzah (roasted egg) 8. Wine 9. Haggadah

SHAVUOT

1. Suggest to the parents of your students some Torah storybooks that they can read at home together.

2. Plan a Shavuot lunch at synagogue for families after the service.

3. Ask each family to bring one house plant to your synagogue to decorate the bimah for Shavuot. They can bring one from home or buy one.

Shavuot Family Readings

The holiday of Shavuot celebrates the place of Torah in Jewish life. On Shavuot eve, traditional Jews stay up all night in the synagogue reading Torah and studying together. According to legend, on this night the heavens open, so prayer will have an especially good chance of reaching God.

Here are excerpts from some traditional sources to study with your children.

• • • • • • • • • •

People used to ask a famous rabbi, "Why is Shavuot called the festival of the giving of our Torah?" The rabbi answered, "The giving of the Torah was on Shavuot. The receiving must happen every day of the year."

As the people of Israel stood before Sinai, the voice thundered, "I am Adonai your God!" "Your" is used in the singular, said our sages, so that each person shall understand that although the voice spoke to everybody, yet it spoke to each person alone.

When the Children of Israel were gathered before Mount Sinai, God hesitated. Although the Israelites wanted the Torah, God foresaw that they might be unfaithful to its teachings. "What will be your surety for this most precious possession?" God asked.

The Israelites replied, "All our gold and silver we give as a pledge."

"The wealth of the world does not measure to one line of Torah," God answered.

Thereupon the Israelites declared, "Our ancestors, Abraham, Isaac, and Jacob are our assurance to you."

"Your ancestors are My debtors and cannot be your surety," was the answer.

Then the Israelites offered, "We give You our children in pledge."

"These I accept as surety," said God. And Israel responded, "We shall teach them diligently to our children, and to our children's children after them."

THINGS TO TALK ABOUT

Discuss the nature of the Torah with your children. (The Torah is more than a holy object. Its teachings must be read and studied and applied to our daily lives. It is a body of knowledge to be used.)

Choose a story in the Torah that you particularly like and read it to your children.

Family Education Experience (Shavuot), *My Jewish Year*, Behrman House, Inc.